NO. 6, WINTER 1997

NEW DIRECTIONS FOR SCHOOL LEADERSHIP

Educating the Throw-Away Children

What We Can Do to Help Students at Risk

RICHARD H. ACKERMAN
University of Massachusetts Lowell
Harvard Graduate School of Education
EDITOR-IN-CHIEF

JOYCE TAYLOR GIBSON
University of Massachusetts Lowell

EDITOR

EDUCATING THE THROW-AWAY CHILDREN:
WHAT WE CAN DO TO HELP STUDENTS AT RISK
Joyce Taylor Gibson (ed.)
New Directions for School Leadership, No. 6, Winter 1997
Richard H. Ackerman, Editor-in-Chief

Microfilm copies of issues and articles are available in 16 mm and 35 mm, as well as microfiche in 105 mm, through University Microfilms Inc., 300 North Zeeb Road, Ann Arbor, Michigan 48106-1346.

ISSN 1089-5612   ISBN 0-7879-9881-8

NEW DIRECTIONS FOR SCHOOL LEADERSHIP is part of The Jossey-Bass Education Series and is published quarterly by Jossey-Bass Inc., Publishers, 350 Sansome Street, San Francisco, California 94104-1342.

SUBSCRIPTIONS: Please see Ordering Information on p. iv.
EDITORIAL CORRESPONDENCE should be sent to Richard Ackerman, The Principals' Center, Harvard Graduate School of Education, 336 Gutman Library, Cambridge, MA, 02138.

Jossey-Bass Web address: http://www.josseybass.com

Printed in the United States of America on acid-free recycled paper containing 100 percent recovered waste paper, of which at least 20 percent is postconsumer waste.

The International Network of Principals' Centers

The International Network of Principals' Centers sponsors *New Directions for School Leadership* as part of its commitment to strengthening leadership at the individual school level through professional development for leaders. The Network has a membership of principals' centers, academics, and practitioners in the United States and overseas and is open to all groups and institutions committed to the growth of school leaders and the improvement of schools. The Network currently functions primarily as an information exchange and support system for member centers in their efforts to work directly with school leaders in their communities. Its office is in the Principals' Center at the Harvard Graduate School of Education.

The Network offers these services:

- The International Directory of Principals' Centers features member centers with contact persons, descriptions of center activities, program references, and evaluation instruments.
- The Annual Conversation takes place every spring, when members meet for seminars, workshops, speakers, and to initiate discussions that will continue throughout the year.
- *Newsnotes*, the Network's quarterly newsletter, informs members of programs, conferences, workshops, and special interest items.
- *Reflections*, an annual journal, includes articles by principals, staff developers, university educators, and principals' center staff members.

For further information, please contact:

International Network of Principals' Centers
Harvard Graduate School of Education
336 Gutman Library
Cambridge, MA 02138
(617) 495-9812

Ordering Information

NEW DIRECTIONS FOR SCHOOL LEADERSHIP
This series of paperback books provides principals, superintendents, teachers, and others who exercise leadership at the local level with insight and guidance on the important issues influencing schools and school leadership. Books in the series are published quarterly in Fall, Winter, Spring and Summer and are available for purchase both by subscription and individually.

SUBSCRIPTIONS cost $52.00 for individuals (a savings of 35 percent over single-copy prices) and $105.00 for libraries. Prices subject to change. There are no shipping and handling charges on subscriptions.

SINGLE COPIES cost $25.00 plus shipping. There will be handling charges on billed orders. Call the 800 number below for more information.

SINGLE COPIES AVAILABLE FOR SALE
SL1   Every Teacher as a Leader: Realizing the Potential of Teacher Leadership, *Gayle Moller, Marilyn Katzenmeyer*
SL2   Boundary Crossings: Educational Partnerships and School Leadership, *Paula A. Cordeiro*
SL3   Schools for Everyone: A New Perspective on Inclusion, *Elizabeth A. Herbert*
SL4   Students Taking the Lead: The Challenges and Rewards of Empowering Youth in Schools, *Judith A. Boccia*
SL5   On Being a Principal: The Rewards and Challenges of School Leadership, *Gordon A. Donaldson Jr.*
SL6   Educating the Throw-Away Children: What We Can Do to Help Students at Risk, *Joyce Taylor Gibson*

QUANTITY DISCOUNTS ARE AVAILABLE. Please contact Jossey-Bass Periodicals for information at 1-415-433-1740.

TO ORDER, CALL 1-800-956-7739 or 1-415-433-1767
. . . and visit our website at http://www.josseybass.com

Contents

*What environmental factors create throw-away children?
What might challenge educators to examine their commitment
to at-risk children? This introductory chapter addresses these
questions and encourages collaboration as a means to prevent
children from dropping out of school and leaving the life of
learning.*

1

Rekindling the spirits of throw-away children

Joyce Taylor Gibson

THIS VOLUME CONSISTS of chapters written by school leaders passionately committed to the children, faculty, and communities they serve. The work is not casual; you will be able to feel the energy, love, and power the writers exude. Most of them blend practical strategies and research, undergirded by the day-to-day experiences that feed both. On first reading, they struck me as compassionate and personal. The authors seem most concerned with rekindling the burning hearts and minds of educators. Though impersonal and mechanical systems relentlessly try to snuff it out, this is the internal fire needed to save throw-away children. Though their backgrounds are diverse, these authors want to accomplish things by collaborating with all who embrace their vision of caring about, connecting with, and educating the throw-away children that others consider ineducable, unwanted, and a drag on the system. They are a new breed of change masters adept at taking risks, collaborating, finding resources, and persuading others of the value and meaning of their work.

NEW DIRECTIONS FOR SCHOOL LEADERSHIP, NO. 6, WINTER 1997 © JOSSEY-BASS PUBLISHERS

They describe safe, structured school communities where high expectations for achievement and caring for the whole child are standard, where mutual respect and honest communication are the norm rather than the exception, and where the adults understand that they may be the only anchor students have. More than anything, the chapters in this volume allow school leaders to observe the deep faith and trust educators can have in each other through their collective experiences and their quest to serve learners within the traditional school structure, as well as in more creative institutions. All this brings hope for the children, the schools, and the larger community of learners.

Taking responsibility for throw-away children

Too many educators give up teaching children too easily. When they do, the results are children with wounded spirits whose natural curiosity about life and learning is lost. Ironically, this happens most often with the children who need our help the most—those who are so different from us that they seem foreign and out of place, who live in a world unfamiliar to us. We are quite capable of rekindling the spirit in their hearts and minds, but we need to be committed to it. By getting to know our students, by bringing to them our own qualities of compassion, humility, and respect, educators open the door to a deeper process of learning in which we can all engage.

But first, we have to acknowledge our personal responsibility for throw-away children. Many educators today fail to take full responsibility for how their actions and attitudes affect students. They distance themselves by imposing policies and practices of yesteryear that were never designed for today's school populations. More often than not, they were never designed for children at all.

Throw-away children are those who, by our narrow definition of such things, fail to make satisfactory academic progress, do not behave well in class, do not do as they are told, or refuse to play the school game as we dictate. They are, in other words, the special-needs kids, the language-minority kids, the disruptive kids, the pregnant kids, the emotionally disturbed kids, the absent-more-than-present kids, the talk-back-to-the-teacher kids, even the quiet, passive kids. These are the potential dropouts, our at-risk youth. They have many names and labels, but they have in common the absence of a significant attachment—either at home or at school—to a caring adult in their lives, an adult who will give them the time, attention, care, and direction they need to flourish.

In a landmark comprehensive study of adolescent behavior, medical researchers interviewed twelve thousand teenagers and came up with startling yet welcome news: youngsters with strong emotional ties to the adults in their lives, particularly parents, were least likely to have health problems or to engage in high-risk behaviors, regardless of family income, race, education, family structure, parental work status, or amount of time spent with parents. Furthermore, "feeling that at least one teacher or adult at school treats them fairly also protected teenagers against every health risk measured except pregnancy—this factor was more important than class size or any particular curriculum" (Foreman, 1997, p. A11). But instead of being that one adult, many educators blame the plight of throw-away kids on school policies, union rules, school board decisions, or what the parents are not doing. All these excuses push students so far away from school that they are lost to any learning environment. Then *they* are blamed for their own circumstances, even as they lose confidence and faith in adults and begin to depend solely on each other.

Hank Levin (Levin, Hopfenberg, and Associates, 1993) calls these young people "children in at-risk situations." I like this description because, unlike the label "at-risk children," it implies that their circumstances are not of their own making and in fact are beyond their control. How can so many educators in so many systems ignore their responsibilities to these children? Is our fear of not being able to help so great that it paralyzes us? Are we so entrenched in our old ways that it is too much trouble to change our own behaviors to meet their needs? Or are we just trying the same old strategies and getting the same old outcomes?

In *The Power of Their Ideas* (1995), educator Deborah Meier speaks of the reaction of other educators who come to visit her school and marvel at the more than twenty years of success she and her staff have had with New York City's throw-away children: "It is hard to convince people that what we do at Central Park East or Central Park Secondary School is reproducible by others—*in their own way*. People often have a whole string of 'well, buts' for why our situation is different from theirs. . . . But the secret ingredient is wanting it badly enough" (pp. 37, 38).

Wanting it badly enough means trying harder and working smarter to help these children succeed in school. In *Moral Leadership* (1992, p. 8), Sergiovanni challenges educators to work smarter by changing their mindscapes, which he describes as "the mental pictures in our heads about how the world works . . . they program what we believe counts, create our own realities, and provide a basis for decisions." School leaders must move beyond their traditional mindscapes to address the unique school needs of children in at-risk situations.

The Office of Educational Research and Improvement, which conducts research in ten regional laboratories throughout the country, said in a major report (1987, p. 1) that there "is no greater educational problem in our nation than improving the educational opportunities and outcomes for students who are placed at risk of educational failure. The vast majority are students who are poor and reside in the inner city, rural areas, or on Indian reservations." The urgency of the problem is clear, for there have been no significant changes since that report. When we as educators give up too easily, it seems we are looking for a quick fix so as to get the problems behind us. We want to cure these children of whatever makes them different and difficult so we can continue to work with minimal disruptions to our routines. But although many throw-away children can improve relatively quickly, others need more time to manage and cope with school and community challenges. Learning a second language, coping with poverty, or reconciling life on the reservation with the culture of the city takes time, support, and great effort, not a quick fix.

I am reminded of a discussion in Thomas Moore's *Care of the Soul* (1992, pp. 18–19): "A major difference between care and cure is that cure implies the end of trouble. If you are cured, you don't have to worry about whatever was bothering you. But care has a sense of ongoing attention." Ongoing attention is one of the keys to turning a child's life from disaster to promise. Without it, the throw-aways of today become the dropouts of tomorrow.

Candidates for dropping out

Children in at-risk situations are prime candidates for dropping out of school. Dropout rates are calculated in so many ways by states and schools using such varied methods of data collection that reliable results on a national level are nearly impossible to acquire. Nonetheless, the Center for Research on Effective Schooling for Disadvantaged Students, which specifically focuses on scientifically studying and evaluating what works with at-risk students, estimates that 20 to 40 percent of our country's children are placed at risk for educational failure. Researchers believe these numbers may be rising due to "increased immigration, poverty, family instability and divorce, teenage pregnancy and violence" (Wood, 1994, p. 188).

Research on school-related factors reveals that poor academic performance is the single strongest predictor of dropping out (Office of Educational Research and Improvement Urban Superintendents Network, 1987; Hess, Well, Prindle, and Kaplan, 1987; Wood, 1994): "Students who repeated one or more grades were twice as likely to drop out than those who had never been held back, and those who repeated more than one grade were four times as likely to leave school before completion" (Wood, 1994, p. 3).

Poor academic performance has many causes. It can be school-related but may have to do with the other three types of factors: student-related (such as the student's personal activities and habits), family-related (such as the degree and nature of parental support), or community-related (such as violence in the neighborhood).

Poverty, however, is a very powerful community-related factor that has an impact on dropping out like no other.

"When socioeconomic factors are controlled for, the differences across racial, ethnic, geographic, and other demographic lines blur" (Office of Educational Research and Improvement Urban Superintendents Network, 1987, p. 5). This means that children in poverty, regardless of their other circumstances, drop out more often than their peers who are not so poor. Relieving the impact of poverty should therefore be a priority for all educators working with at-risk populations. Understanding the nature of what I call this twenty-first century poverty is imperative if we are to connect with the children. But Martin Haberman, renowned American teacher educator, warns that today's poverty is unlike that of the past: "The cumulative effort of growing up in poverty today produces school-age children who, in many critical ways, do not resemble textbook children" (1993, p. 4).

The message here is that we must get to know what is real, normal, and usual in the children's environment if we are to understand who they are and how to help them. Haberman said children in the new poverty often face the following:

- Growing up without adults they can trust
- Living in communities where violence and abuse of human beings is high
- Experiencing feelings of despair and lack of hope—hope for a better life beyond their troubled lives
- Witnessing their family's inhuman treatment from the bureaucracies that were established to help them
- Resigning themselves to a state of powerlessness, being at the whim of some other authority outside their families (pp. 3–6)

This glimpse at poverty offers insights for developing strategies and programs that educators can use to work toward a more positive school experience for children of poverty. Is it really so hard to understand that as the world changes we must change as well? New poverty and different school populations require new strategies and educators with new insights and resources to solve the challenges of this new century. Public educators are still responsible for any child who attends school—and new mindscapes are imperative for the survival of these children and our schools.

About this issue

The number of successful programs for children in at-risk situations is increasing, and they offer opportunity and hope for many. But though there are not enough in any one state or country for us to stop recruiting for change, thousands of students in poverty or at risk in other ways are finding success in schools and becoming contributing members of society.

The chapters that follow demonstrate that educators can personalize the schooling process and facilitate students' growth into intelligent, resourceful problem solvers of the future. Here is a glimpse of the types of roles some educators play to support throw-away children.

In Vancouver, Native Indian educator Lorna Williams became the first administrator from her culture to be hired to address the historical repressive treatment of native children in the public schools; her story is about the struggles and triumphs of influencing a whole system to be responsive to children previously educated on the reservations. Yet her struggle is not unlike that of Peggy C. Kirby, university professor and board member of Louisiana's first charter school, one of the only educational refuges for expelled middle school children. Each of these leaders has a vision for the education of forgotten children, and each has witnessed progress, yet they understand that their efforts must continue, especially team building, assessment, and communication with community partners who have joined them in their work.

In Boston, a public school caters in the evenings to teenagers who attempt to manage every trauma imaginable that hinders finishing high school; director Ferdinand Fuentes and his largely part-time staff bring a caring agenda and a network of community resources to help adolescents keep their promise to "get my high school diploma." Not far away in the Merrimack Valley is a high school dropout program in which the faculty and the director, Karen Moore, offer weekly opportunities for student participation in decision making at the policy and practical levels of the school. Mutual respect and accountability are common to both these school communities, which means that school leaders have to practice what they believe on a daily basis.

Diane Jackson and Myra Chang Thompson take us into the world of individual children, focusing on teacher efficacy, research-based practices that work, and feedback—from children, parents, and assessments—to guide their work with throw-away children. Jackson focuses on a child who decides that he will no longer do his homework. However, a step-by-step confidence-building process that she teaches him reignites his interests and reconnects him to school. Thompson's case story is about a special-needs child who learns to compensate for his reading disability and is not allowed to give up. These school leaders had the confidence and competence to defy the odds by steadily focusing on opportunities and goals for each child—not on the obstacles, pressures, or politics of the school environment.

Six years ago Chery S. Wagonlander opened a school that combines the best practices and best research to bring dropouts back into the educational system. By creating a community where faculty and students participate in the action research about their model program, a level of understanding and accountability about the educational process was developed beyond their original aspirations.

Self-connection, sensing one's purpose, and helping children do the same in their everyday work is the theme of the final chapter in this journal. According to Pamela Gerloff, staying connected to one's true purpose will open vistas to break down the conditions that lead to throw-away children. Time for reflection and review of one's work is critical to continuous growth and grounding of the true self, all of which is important to staying connected to ourselves.

The work of these practitioners is exciting, even awe-inspiring in some cases, yet they would have the reader know that they are all still learning and growing from their current experiences and do not see themselves as experts. But they are far along enough to want to share the commitment, confidence, and pride in what they and their communities have accomplished to date.

References

Foreman, J. "Study Links Parental Bond to Teenage Well-Being." *Boston Globe*, Sept. 10, 1997, A1, A11.

Haberman, M. "Diverse Contexts for Teaching." In M. J. O'Hair and S. J. Odell (eds.), *Diversity and Teaching: Teacher Education Yearbook I*. Fort Worth, Tex.: Harcourt Brace, 1993, 3–6.

Hess, G. A. Jr., Well, E., Prindle, C. P., and Kaplan, B. "'Where's Room 185?' How Schools Can Reduce Their Dropout Problem." *Education and Urban Society*, 1987, *19*(3), 330–355.

Levin, H., Hopfenberg, W. S., and Associates. *The Accelerated Schools Resource Guide*. San Francisco: Jossey-Bass, 1993.

Meier, D. *The Power of Their Ideas*. Boston: Beacon Press, 1995.

Office of Educational Research and Improvement Urban Superintendents Network. *Dealing with Dropouts: The Urban Superintendents' Call to Action*. Washington, D.C.: Office of Educational Research and Improvement, 1987.

Moore, T. *Care of the Soul*. New York: HarperCollins, 1992.

Sergiovanni, T. J. *Moral Leadership*. San Francisco: Jossey-Bass, 1992.

Wood, L. A. "An Unintended Impact of One Grading Practice." *Urban Education*, 1994, *29*(2), 188–201.

JOYCE TAYLOR GIBSON, *assistant professor of education at the University of Massachusetts, Lowell, focuses her teaching and research on leadership for change, cultural diversity, and family-school partnerships.*

In Louisiana, the concerned citizens of Jefferson Parish, a professor of education, and criminal justice workers took advantage of legislation allowing the creation of a different kind of independent public school. They proposed a school for expelled middle school children, and a public school opened its doors with the unanimous support of the community to address the academic and social needs of these throw-away children. The author describes the evolution of the school and the lessons she and her colleagues learned about building a new school focused on an old problem.

2

The most at-risk of students at risk

Peggy C. Kirby

"AT RISK" IS A POPULAR PHRASE used to describe the thousands of youth in danger of dropping out of school or being excluded from school involuntarily. Each year, scores of programs are implemented to target the at-risk child. Unfortunately, most such interventions concentrate on the younger learner or the young adult. Accelerated Schools, Comer Schools, and Success for All, for example, begin in and focus on the elementary schools. Essential Schools and School-to-Work programs typically target the high school student. The middle school student (herein referred to as the "young adolescent") is perhaps the student at greatest risk, yet few specific programs are designed to save the child in the middle.

NEW DIRECTIONS FOR SCHOOL LEADERSHIP, NO. 6, WINTER 1997 © JOSSEY-BASS PUBLISHERS

Middle schools at risk

In Louisiana, children may legally quit school at age sixteen. Many sixteen-year-old dropouts are two to four years behind grade level. Although they should be sophomores and juniors, many never even made it to high school. They have experienced repeated failure as a result of poor academic performance and behavior problems. Often these two causes are linked, as with the sixth grader who acts out to avoid exposure as a nonreader. The severity of the problem is compounded further by the volatile developmental changes that plague all young adolescents. Physically, emotionally, socially, and cognitively, the ages from about eleven to sixteen are without doubt the most difficult time of growth and adjustment; for too many children, it is the point at which they are most at risk.

The discipline records of local school districts support the contention that young adults are at greatest risk. Middle school students are suspended and expelled in far greater proportions than students at other levels. In some Louisiana school districts, as many as one in four students are suspended at the middle level each academic year. In Jefferson Parish, the first charter school opened in Fall 1996; it was created to serve the middle school child who had been expelled from the public school for chronic discipline problems. The number of applicants far exceeded the number of seats; desperate parents pleaded with school administrators to give their child this new start.

The concept of middle-level improvement has attracted wide attention in the greater New Orleans area. A number of factors heighten the concern. In addition to the disproportionately high rate of discipline offenses at the period of most rapid physical and psychological change, young adolescents are least likely to have teachers specifically trained to meet their unique needs. In spite of national reports urging special training for middle school teachers and administrators, such training remains insufficient or nonexistent (Scales and McEwin, 1994). The short-lived upper elementary teacher certification in Louisiana is scheduled for phase-out in the year 2000. So few teachers in training elected this level that a separate certification would guarantee a severe shortage of eligible teachers. Thus, after the year 2000 teachers again will be certified to teach at the middle grades by obtaining either elementary (K–8) or secondary (8–12) certification.

Nevertheless, efforts to focus on middle school improvement have been embraced in southeast Louisiana. The Jefferson Community School, a charter alternative school, was created by a coalition of concerned citizens, educators, and criminal justice workers who recognized the crisis in middle-level schools. St. Bernard Parish Public Schools also recognized the need for an alternative to expulsion and planned to create its own alternative middle school. The Louisiana Board of Elementary and Secondary Education supported a course for middle school improvement at the University of New Orleans in Summer 1996. Although the course is not required in any certification program, enrollment was at capacity, and students requested a second offering. Goals 2000 and Louisiana LEARN projects in Jefferson and St. Bernard Parish have specifically targeted middle school improvement since 1994. Orleans Parish recently implemented an annual middle schools conference to assist educators in understanding and assisting the young adolescent.

There is no doubt, then, that concern about the young adolescent is intense even when solutions are scarce. As we lose the war on drugs, teen pregnancies are skyrocketing, adolescent suicides are increasing, and children are dropping out of school. Our solution is not to punish the troubled youth through exclusion but to recognize their crisis and become experts on their developmental needs.

Few teachers choose the middle level as their preferred placement. Fewer still are trained to be there. Many middle school principals have little or no experience as middle school teachers. Unlike their secondary and elementary counterparts, who have their own professional leadership organizations (National Association for Secondary School Principals and National Association for Elementary School Principals), middle school leaders are a less unified group. The National Middle School Association (NMSA), however, has published a beliefs treatise for general middle level educators (Lipsitz, Jackson, and Austin, 1997) that offers some guidance to the middle school principal, and the Task Force on Education of Young Adolescents (1989) of the Carnegie Council produced what is considered the definitive document on best middle school practice.

Developmentally appropriate middle schools

Given the obstacles to success, what can we do to save the at-risk middle school child? We have known since 1989 that eight essential elements constitute effective middle-level practice:

- Smaller communities for learning within the larger middle school
- A common core of high-level knowledge and skills
- Instruction organized to incur success
- Empowered teachers and administrators
- Special training for middle-grade teachers
- Better health and fitness programs
- Families reengaged in their children's education
- Connections with the larger community (Task Force on Education of Young Adolescents, 1989)

Recent studies have offered research support for these practices (such as Felner, Kasak, Mulhall, and Flowers, 1997; Seghers, 1996). Unfortunately, these components are interdependent: implementation of only select components will not yield improvements in student performance (Lipsitz, Jackson, and Austin, 1997). Success at the middle level requires a concerted effort by teachers, administrators, parents, and other community members. Shared belief in a middle school philosophy is the key to improved middle schools.

The National Middle School Association (1997) recently updated its philosophy statement in *This We Believe: Developmentally Responsive Middle Level Schools*. It suggests that middle school programs, like good early childhood programs, must be based on what is "developmentally appropriate" for the learner. Building on developmental psychology, the association proposes practices that acknowledge the young adolescent's natural needs for acceptance, control, challenge, relevance, and identity. On trying to understand the failure of so many middle schools to meet the needs of young adolescents, we found nearly total incongruence between what we know to be developmentally appropriate and actual school and classroom practices.

The typical middle school: a developmental mismatch

The typical middle school in southeast Louisiana had not by 1996 met the recommendations of either the Carnegie Task Force or the NMSA. Indeed, in my work with the three school districts I observed practices directly in conflict with what I knew to be emotionally, cognitively, physically, and socially appropriate for the developing young adolescent. Rather than a unified core curriculum, students learned disjointed subjects with an emphasis on basic skills. There was no social focus such as smaller learning environments as recommended by the Carnegie Task Force, nor were there exploratory classes or advisory periods as recommended by NMSA. When adolescents needed relevance and integration, their curriculum remained meaningless and fragmented.

Instructional practices also violated what is psychologically appropriate for the young adolescent. Although such students are in a period of development that requires peer approval and support, teachers rarely provided opportunities for peer-assisted teaching, group work, or student-centered discussions. Computers, a tool for learning that young adolescents find challenging and accepting, were used primarily for remediation and reward. Students who could benefit most from this alternative teaching form were least likely to have access to it (Kirby, 1992).

Perhaps in no area was there greater lack of awareness of student needs than in the use of time and space. Middle school classes typically began around 7:30 A.M. (Elementary and high school students began after 8:00 A.M.) The middle school day ended as early as 2:30 P.M. Any parent of any preteen knows that this is the stage of development when children begin sleeping later. Working parents also know how difficult it is to find appropriate supervision for eleven- to fifteen-year-olds after school. What middle schools were doing was wakening children too soon and sending them home too early—often to empty houses. Further, the young adolescent's day was divided into six or seven fixed time periods with no flexibility for longer projects or more difficult learning.

Teachers' use of time was also inappropriate. They had one planning period for individual planning but were not scheduled for common planning times with other teachers of the same subjects or the same students. Thus, any expectations that subjects would be integrated and relevant were frustrated.

The adolescent's need for identity was further confounded by the use of space. Students were expected to collect everything they owned every forty-eight minutes and carry it with them to the next location. Although students had lockers, they had no desk, classroom, or common group of classmates that they could call their own. Added to this depersonalization was the humiliation of the natural forgetfulness that plagues young adolescents. Allowed to go to their lockers only two or three times a day, they were often chastised in class for not having the right textbook, notebook, or teacher-mandated color of ink. Adults, whose sense of responsibility and organization are far keener, would never choose to spend an entire day working under such constrictions.

The subject matter fragmentation and teacher isolation in middle schools was perpetuated by lack of teamwork. Teachers set their own rules for behavior in the classrooms, on the schoolyard, and in the cafeteria. Students had to adapt to a new set of rules and consequences more than seven times a day. There was no single adult to whom most students could go for advice or encouragement. In fact, I observed some teachers who did not know the names of all of their students by the end of the school year. Parents and community mentors were rarely involved in any direct way with students.

The Jefferson Community School

Given this wealth of information about what should happen (and what actually does) in middle schools, and given the increasing number of dropouts and expulsions, I longed to create a developmentally appropriate school for the most at-risk middle-level students. That opportunity came in 1996, when the Louisiana legislature passed a law allowing the creation of a different kind of independent public school. An independent group, consisting of at least three certified educators, could propose a quasi-public school (or schools) to the board of the public school district in which the charter school would reside. The charter school population had to reflect the same or greater proportion of at-risk students as the chartering district. Thus, the elite magnet school allowed by some state charter school laws was not possible in Louisiana. Perhaps for this reason, only three charter schools opened in Louisiana in Fall 1996.

As a former middle school teacher, professor of school leadership, and frequent collaborator with the Jefferson Parish Public School System, I was asked by the superintendent to write the proposal for the Jefferson Community School (JCS). I worked with the school district and the district attorney's staff to propose a developmentally responsive middle school supported by "community/ interagency cooperation, freedom from bureaucratic constraints, strong teacher efficacy, and a combined behavior management/academic approach . . ." (Jefferson Coalition for Alternative Schools, 1997, p. 2). JCS goals included a juvenile delinquency prevention program, an accelerated curriculum, variety in instructional strategies, a safe, alternative setting, access to social services, developmentally appropriate use of time and space, positive role models, monitored behavioral management plans, and ongoing instructional diagnosis and planning.

The specific strategies deemed developmentally appropriate and different from the typical middle schools from which these students were expelled included the following:

- Integrated subject matter through teacher teaming
- Full exploratory program

- Advisory periods for more personal adult contact
- Student-centered approaches to instruction
- Integrated physical and mental health education
- Diverse learning style approaches
- Block scheduling
- Team planning time
- Later school day
- Student ownership of classrooms, limited movement between classes, separate teacher offices
- Computer lab
- Consistent rules of behavior
- Interagency advisory board
- Active parent involvement
- Community mentoring

JCS, founded by the Jefferson Coalition for Alternative Schools, was the first Louisiana charter school to open its doors. With the unanimous support of the Jefferson Parish Public School Board and superintendent, as well as the district attorney, Parish Council, and private businesses, the school opened with a state-of-the-art computer lab, a full-time social worker, and a student-teacher ratio of 15:1. All students who had been expelled from any of the parish's sixteen middle schools during the prior school year were invited to attend. Although these students had been excluded during the 1995–1996 school term, they were eligible to return to their regular public schools in Fall 1996. Many parents, however, saw the charter school as a fresh start for their children. Because capacity was limited to a hundred students, seventy-five were randomly selected from the 170 students who applied. The remaining twenty-five seats were reserved for students who would be expelled early in the new school year.

Although not all strategies in the proposal were implemented in the first year, the staff attempted to comply with the changes in curriculum, instruction, and discipline. The developers referred to the school as an "experiment in progress" as programs were created, evaluated, and revised.

Once the proposal was accepted by the local and state school boards, my role at JCS was as a member of the Coalition for Alternative Schools (the board of directors) and chair of the executive committee. The seven-member executive committee met monthly to provide assistance to the school staff. I also visited the school on a weekly basis, observing classes, discussing concerns with the principal, assisting with staff development, and creating the exploratory program. I was an unpaid consultant with a keen interest in the school's success. Dismayed by my own experiences as a middle school teacher and frustrated with my older son's torment at the hands of uncaring middle school teachers, I felt compelled to make this school work. For me, this was the birth of a child who was long overdue.

Several obstacles had to be overcome for the "true" middle school concept to be achieved. The changes in the structure of the school day and use of space were embraced by teachers. Each teacher had a semiprivate office equipped with a Pentium computer, laser printer, and adequate shelving. Rolling carts were purchased to help teachers move their supplies and equipment from class to class. Students immediately appreciated the new furniture and a desk to call their own. Desktop graffiti was only a minor problem. After much compromising about the arrangement of desks, teachers and students established an acceptable routine for class changes. Students left their home classrooms only for physical education classes, to use the computer lab, and for lunch.

The later school day proved to be problematic for some students. Although the first class began at 9:00 A.M., many students had to awaken long before that in order to catch the school bus. The large district size meant that the distance to school for some students was quite long. Also, because only a limited number of buses could serve the hundred-student school, some students traveled for as long as an hour and half twice each day. By October of the first year, seventeen parents had decided to place their children back at their regular schools to avoid the long rides.

There was no shortage of students to replace those who left. Students who had been expelled between August and October had no alternative. They could not return to their regular schools until the following August, they could not enroll in another public school in the district, and they would fail for the year if they stayed at home. These students were accepted into the charter school as space became available. The school remained at capacity for the entire school year.

Another major obstacle during the first year was inexperience with teaming. The teachers had not worked in a similar setting and had no nearby models to observe. Some had little or no experience with the subjects they were assigned to teach. Although a separate planning period was established for team meetings, some teachers were more comfortable planning on their own; for others, differences in personality made working together difficult. Not until the end of the school year did the staff attempt its first integrated thematic unit. Governance issues remained unclear to many. The responsibilities of teachers versus administrators under the site-based management had to be negotiated, as did the relationship between the school administration and the charter governing board. And, of course, this was the first charter school in the state, so knowing what charter schools could and could not do was always in question.

School-community collaboration and school-home cooperation were not emphasized during the first year. The social worker did a commendable job of getting to know the students and their families and of seeking external assistance where needed. The small student population made it possible for everyone to know all students. When problems arose, a specific adult could be called upon to help the student with whom she had developed a rapport. In effect, all teachers, the principal, the secretary, and the custodian committed themselves to keeping these youngsters in school.

A local hospital became a sponsor of the school, donating funds for a science lab and basketball court, as well as volunteer help. A nearby high school sponsored a Junior ROTC for JCS students. The intended mentoring program did not materialize, nor did significant parent involvement.

Two middle school experts conducted an independent evaluation of JCS in March 1997. They were asked to determine how successful the school staff had been in implementing the objectives of the charter proposal. They created a fourteen-item Likert scale questionnaire that was completed by all twelve members of the faculty and staff—seven teachers, one teacher assistant, the principal, the social worker, the secretary, and the custodian. Each item assessed the level of success in implementing one objective. After completing the questionnaire, each individual was interviewed by one or both evaluators. In open-ended responses, participants offered their opinions on the successes and failures of the first year and solutions for the next year. The evaluators also observed each teacher at least once for a whole class period.

The evaluation confirmed that access to social services and a variety of instructional methods were available to JCS students. Evaluators found the staff to be uniformly caring, dedicated, and hard-working. They were surprised by the considerable financial support for instructional supplies and equipment. Responses to items concerning school governance, curriculum, and safety also were generally positive.

The written evaluation revealed three areas in need of improvement: individual adult-student support, individualized behavior management plans, and positive linkages to the community. Evaluators' observations in classrooms revealed rather traditional approaches to instruction and class sizes that they perceived as too large. Observers suggested that class size be reduced, the advisory and exploratory programs improved, and teachers provided training in instructional and behavior management methods in alternative education.

In response to the evaluation, two major changes were implemented for the second year. Although the budget did not permit hiring additional teachers to reduce class size, the board was able to secure funding to hire three additional teacher assistants. Thus, each class would have at least one teacher and one assistant at all times. Also, an additional week of in-service training (with pay) was planned for all staff prior to the beginning of the next school year. Topics of discussion would include teamwork, alternative methods of instruction, discipline programs, and school-based management.

Other assessments of the success of JCS include the enrollment figures and test performance. Of the seventy-five students who started in August 1996, twenty-five (34 percent) failed to complete the school year at JCS. As explained earlier, seventeen of these were transferred back to their regular schools at their parents' request due to lengthy travel times to and from school. Another twenty-three who were admitted after August left or were asked to leave. Student expulsions resulted only when repeated in-school suspensions failed or when students committed more severe offenses, such as distribution of controlled substances on campus. Perhaps the most important bit of data is that the 1996–1997 term ended with ninety-eight students who would not have been in school at all if not for JCS.

Thirty-six seventh-grade students (73 percent) passed the state-administered criterion-referenced test for language arts in May 1997; twenty-one (43 percent) passed the math portion of the state test. Of those who finished the school year at JCS, 57 percent passed all subjects. Five more attended summer school; 62 percent were promoted to the next grade. The staff met to determine which of the ninety-eight students would benefit from moving back to the regular schools and which would benefit from completing their next year at JCS. Forty parents were encouraged to allow their children to stay at JCS.

Finally, students themselves provided the most poignant and revealing testimony about the successes and failures of our first year in trying to save the child in the middle. The two language arts teachers asked students at the end of the year to write about their experiences at JCS. Here, in their own words, spelling, punctuation, and grammar, are some of the students' assessments:

One of my best experiences at this school is the attention from the teachers, they aren't like most teachers at other schools. . . . RESPECT is wanted every second of the day.

I look at some people who are sixteen and up and still are in middle school, and I know I don't want to turn out like that. I want to return to regular school and try my hardest to stay in school and pass. If I get expelled (which I will try not to let happen) I will try to finish the year at JCS, and I will try to be promoted to 8th grade and I will be only one year behind. And that's better than nothing!

Ever since I came to JCS it was like a whole new education for me. But before I came here it was like trouble slapped me in the face every time I walked into [previous school]. Here at JCS the teachers take time out of their busy schedule to help you out.

I used to fight a lot but when I got here they taught me to talk about what made me want to fight rather than fight. At first I didn't want to come here, but I didn't have a choice, I'm glad my mom made me come. . . .

[My teacher] has helped me with my work. . . . She knows that sometimes I try real hard but still don't understand stuff. [She] does not let other people make fun of me and works with me until I get it. My whole attitude has changed about school work, and I'm glad I have changed.

If I pass the seventh grade I will teach my brothers and sisters to do right and never come to Jefferson Community School because I don't want my family to face [the same teacher mentioned in the previous excerpt].

I am in the 8th grade. My first couple of months at JCS, I gave everyone hell. I always thought that since people considered me as a bad child, I might as well act like one. I been at JCS since the first day of school. My grades at JCS were pretty fair. The first nine weeks, I made B's and C's. That was the first time that I made B's or C's, that was the first time that I stayed in school to even get a first report card [Dawson and Kreisman, 1997].

Lessons learned

Given our own observations, the evaluator's findings, the enrollment and test data, and the students' narratives, we are left with mixed feelings about our success in saving the child in the middle.

Clearly we have had some success in keeping a large number of at-risk youth in school. We have to acknowledge, however, that we failed to help others. Though we are not so naive as to believe that we should have been 100 percent successful, we do recognize the power of the information we collected in helping us improve our success rate next year. We offer the following advice to those attempting—perhaps against considerable odds—to save the most at-risk of at-risk middle school youth.

1. Select teachers carefully. Subject matter expertise and pedagogical skills are a bonus, but if you have to choose, select teachers committed to the at-risk child first. Those who really believe that all children can learn will themselves learn what they need to succeed with their students.

2. Provide teacher training. Don't expect teachers to know how to work together. If they haven't, they naturally feel threatened when their routines are questioned.

3. Support teachers. To become a team, they need time, resources, and encouragement.

4. Enhance developmental literacy. Ensure that every member of the school team understands what it means to provide developmentally appropriate education (cognitively, emotionally, physically, and morally) for the young adolescent.

5. Know and respect students. To do so, provide individual adult contact and get to know their families. Accept that today's breakthrough may be short-lived. Setbacks are normal with at-risk students, but they too may be temporary.

6. Create an atmosphere for success. Establish an environment that provides safety, order, and consistency.

7. Demand community support. Insist on adequate support for the at-risk student. Do not assume that you can educate the most at-risk students for the same or fewer dollars as the more socially adjusted.

8. Champion your school. To increase the support for and resources of your school, promote it within your community.

9. Keep experimenting. Utilize multiple forms of assessment (such as observation, surveys, standardized tests, external eval-

uations, and self-study), do so continually, and make revisions based on your data.

10. Think democracy. Don't assume that you are responsible for all successes or failures. Have your entire team analyze data, generate alternative solutions, and analyze consequences. Every available person should work for the success of the whole team and the future of the at-risk student in the middle.

My experiences with JCS have not all been positive. As with any child, there are triumphs and setbacks. But my optimism is renewed with the start of the second year. An energetic, caring faculty and an administration with a year of experience under its belt make my presence at JCS rather unnecessary. I will continue, however, to assist in the school's development, hoping that the "terrible twos" don't pertain to my metaphorical child.

Over the summer of 1997, I had the opportunity to interview a professor of education and a teacher union president in Austria. I wanted to know how middle school education there compared to that of the United States. My Austrian colleagues were puzzled by my questions. Yes, they had experienced an increase in drug use among adolescents (one case in the past year, up from none the prior year). But most revealing was the teacher's response to my question about the number of expulsions of young adolescents. After I explained that expulsion meant removing a child from school, usually for the remainder of the school term, he stared at me incredulously. "Why would you ever do that?" he wanted to know. "Well," I asked, "how do you deal with persistent behavior problems?" The response: "We work with that child, of course!"

Of course. And until a school like JCS is no longer needed, we too will work with that child.

References

Dawson, N., and Kreisman, J. "What Have We Learned?" Unpublished manuscript. Jefferson Parish, La.: Jefferson Community School, 1997.

Felner, R. D., Kasak, D., Mulhall, P., and Flowers, N. "The Project on High Performance Learning Communities." *Phi Delta Kappan*, 1997, 78(7), 520–527.

Jefferson Coalition for Alternative Schools. *Jefferson Community School: A Charter Alternative Middle School Proposal Submitted to the Jefferson Parish Public School System*. Jefferson Parish, La.: Jefferson Coalition for Alternative Schools, 1997.

Kirby, P. C. "Wealth, Ability, and School Computer Use: A Critical Review." *Unterrichteswwissenschaft*, 1992, *20*(1), 49–59.

Lipsitz, J., Jackson, A. W., and Austin, L. M. "What Works in Middle Grade Reform." *Phi Delta Kappan*, 1997, *78*(7), 517–519.

National Middle School Association. *This We Believe: Developmentally Responsive Middle Level Schools*. Columbus, Ohio: National Middle School Association, 1997.

Scales, P. C., and McEwin, C. K. *The Making of America's Middle School Teachers*. Columbus, Ohio: National Middle School Association and Center for Early Adolescence, 1994.

Seghers, M. "The Effects of Implementation of the Carnegie (1989) Middle School Recommendations in Louisiana Middle Schools." Unpublished doctoral dissertation, Department of Educational Leadership, University of New Orleans, 1996.

Task Force on Education of Young Adolescents. *Turning Points: Preparing American Youth for the 21st Century*. New York: Carnegie Council on Adolescent Development, 1989.

PEGGY C. KIRBY *is professor of educational leadership at the University of New Orleans and chair of the board of directors of Louisiana's first charter school, the Jefferson Community School. She is coauthor with Joseph Blase of* Bringing Out the Best in Teachers: What Effective Principals Do. *She also has written numerous articles on school restructuring, especially at the middle school level.*

An alternative high school program succeeds through developing a framework responsive to the needs of at-risk students by promoting a proactive and empathic school culture that is non-traditional and academically challenging.

3

Creating high academic expectations from a caring commitment

Ferdinand Fuentes

MANY EDUCATORS TODAY are struggling with students who are at risk for numerous reasons. The Downtown Evening Academy, an alternative high school program in Boston, has by no means solved all its students' problems. But by sharing our rationale, core values, and approaches to learning, and by explaining how we learn from students and our understanding of the role of leadership and the management of change, we hope to serve other practitioners in developing programs that affect the lives of so-called throw-away children.

The core values of the academy

The Downtown Evening Academy is an alternative learning environment for students who have been categorized as being at risk or at high risk. A majority of our students are young teen parents, students who have been labeled as dropouts or as having special needs, and others who have a broad array of social circumstances that

NEW DIRECTIONS FOR SCHOOL LEADERSHIP, NO. 6, WINTER 1997 © JOSSEY-BASS PUBLISHERS

impede their development. Our student body also includes those who have had difficulty working within the regular school environment because they cannot adapt to the prescribed roles of traditional learners, to curriculum subject matters, or to the schedules and timetables offered within the majority of Boston high schools. Table 3.1 shows a basic demographic profile of our students.

The core of our school and the foundation of our educational task is centered upon *eleos* and *empatheia*, Greek for compassion and empathy. Compassion is essential to a caring community that seeks to focus on both the content and character of the educational process. It is a commitment to care, to believe in, and to uphold the other (in this case the student) as a person of unique value. Empathy is the capacity and effort to understand the other's circumstances and engage in addressing his or her pain. This empathetic action stems from the process of self-awareness. It allows students and faculty to see themselves, to believe in themselves, to be attuned with the environment. The empathetic dimension is one of the mechanisms by which moral and critical reflections are fostered (Goleman, 1995).

The experience of compassion and empathy was well expressed by the academy's 1997 valedictorian, Cathy Ortega: "At the Academy, the teachers not only believed in me and taught me to believe in myself, they cared for me and for my children, they were teachers, and were also my friends. . . . I now want to continue my education and be a role model for my children" ("Boston Graduates," 1997). Ortega is one of many young student parents affirmed by

Table 3.1. Downtown Evening Academy demographics.

Percentage	Academy Student Profile
70 percent	At or below poverty levels
65 percent	Teen parents
65 percent	Independent living
40 percent	Employed
32 percent	Special education
25 percent	Probation or court involved
20 percent	Transient living situation

the program. This affirmation enabled her to pursue her dream and to set goals to strive for and achieve.

What we do

In addressing the human circumstance through profound, empathetic, proactive engagement, we affirm and involve the student in the process of healing and self-realization. Many of these so-called throw-away kids need mentoring, structure, and an opportunity to see their own potential. As adults we sometimes make simple observations about our students that we fail to affirm and express. That these students still cope and pursue a learning track, despite the social obstacles and pressures, is an asset and a strength. We have to assess and affirm for students what is working in their lives outside the school. Are these students caring and involved parents? Are they employed? Are they coping with serious family illnesses such as AIDS? Are they supporting families or siblings? Are they present in some form in the life of the school, pushing their desire to learn in the midst of the message of hopelessness and negative feedback that they receive?

When we focus on the lives of the students and express a deep caring for them, we grow as educators. This serves as a bridge allowing teachers to cross into the lives of students and become highly effective. This caring is reflected in our attitudes. We say to ourselves, *I wonder what is happening in their lives today. What went well and what went badly?* In other schools these students too often encounter another attitude: *What's wrong with this one?* As one faculty member stated last year, "It is different here at this school. I teach during the day, but here I am able to teach, and am able to get involved in the lives of these kids. I know every one them— their habits, looks, and manner. We talk and share. We are aware when someone is missing and may have something going on in their lives. I have learned to ask what is happening in their lives. I have learned it is not easy for them. I admire them. It is more like family and they got me responding, pushing me to learn."

A major part of our educational role is to accept the students, recognizing their strengths and possibilities, and the realities they face—which are very different from our own. As one student said, "I know you want to help me, but you gotta know where I am coming from, I gotta know you are real." These students, who have survived countless disappointments, are seeking to make a difference in their lives. They are making the extra effort to succeed. That in itself is a critical asset that needs to be affirmed in the life of the student. This process of fostering their own self-reliance and capacity builds upon the sense of hope for the students. School staff have to be willing to work authentically with students as whole persons. Authenticity is the ability to express with clarity what one is, what one stands for, and why one is committed to the mission and task at hand (Sikes, 1989).

From a teaching standpoint, authenticity means becoming vulnerable and human, recognizing and being willing to share our limitations, biases, and attitudes about life, learning, and reality. We need to provide students with a sense of hope and belief about their future. We need to begin from a pedagogy of hope (Freire, 1994), because the poverty these students face teaches them hopelessness (Postman, 1995). This sense of hope and caring serves as a foundation to students, allowing them to believe in themselves and to be partners with the teachers in the process of self-discovery and educational development. Many times, teachers and staff encourage students by telling them that nothing is impossible, hoping they will not be discouraged by the initial obstacles they encounter. Yet we fail to consider that we may be encouraging a student on a goal or path that will ultimately lead to disappointment. There is a fine line between establishing goals and objectives that may seem difficult and establishing illusions that are not grounded enough to allow the student to build upon existing strengths and capacities. Hope, in overwhelmingly difficult conditions, requires that we build upon concrete skills, abilities, and realistic assessments. When one of our students, Millie, thought about getting her Class B driver's license, no one laughed at her; she was a special-education bus driver at the time. We researched the options and helped her explore the goal. She decided she would like to work a forklift, which would increase her income from six dollars an hour to twenty-five. If she pursued the goal, she would be on her way and, as she stated, "off the welfare bandwagon." This was a realistic hope, and it motivated her to actually pursue that goal. This was not the limit of what she could do but the beginning of what could occur. To foster hope is to allow students to dream and envision, to see beyond the current box of learning and constraints of their everyday social reality. The goal Millie sought would be difficult to attain, but built upon an existing strength. She felt confidence in herself and was willing to explore and venture into the unknown. This was a sound beginning that would impact other areas of her life.

Relearning from our students

A major complaint young people have about adults is that we already have the answer to questions that have not yet emerged. We respond proactively without listening first, which is condescending to the student. As teachers and adults, many times we are biased with our own opinions of the student situation. We have learned two key insights at the academy:

1. We are dealing with young adults who are trying to manage adult responsibilities.
2. We have to be able to listen patiently and attentively to what they say.

Many of the stories we hear about our students confirm that their circumstances are complex and cannot be categorized within existing social classifications of abuse, incest, social disorder, depression, and the like. We learned this through many cases that our guidance counselor, a gifted woman with a master's degree in social work and another in psychology, encountered in managing high-risk cases and group home placements with indigent students. A number of us have been exposed to a broad range of complex and difficult human circumstances and family suffering. We thought that nothing would surprise us; yet the complexities of the nineties are very different from previous times and require us to shift to another level of thinking about the everyday lives of our students. Here is a case that taught us about our students' everyday lives.

A nineteen-year-old mom came to the guidance counselor concerned about her graduation. She was living with her boyfriend, her leg was broken, and she was having problems coming to school. She said she was trying to regain her two children, who were in custody of the state because of her drug use, for which she was in therapy. She added she was also coping with her mom's recent death from AIDS. She had not been on speaking terms with her mother because she, the daughter, had brought rape charges against her stepfather when he tried to rape her, an act her mom denied. Nor was this the only rape charge she had filed, as she was dealing with the same situation with her dad. When the guidance counselor asked how she was coping with all this, given the broken leg, she said, "Oh, my boyfriend and me got into a fight and he threw me out the second-floor window, but it's okay now, he is seeking help. Do you think that I can make up the work so I can graduate this year?"

For the next three months the counselor tried to reach out and coordinate other support for her. A major premise of the support systems in the school is that we need to provide a safe haven that promotes self-reliance through concrete, responsible action on the part of the students. The counselor was able to provide the resources, but the student needed to follow up on all the support systems and therapy that were made available. One contribution of our guidance counselor is that she motivates students to be self-reliant and to understand that they are able to make choices. Our school staff members promote a culture that seeks to do away with the victim mentality. The students' social circumstances and limitations are also framed and presented as areas of motivation, maturity, and challenge that will allow for their growth.

The case just described portrays the complexity that students are facing. The school is ill equipped to address such a variety of social needs, but though we cannot eliminate poverty, housing and health care problems, and social turmoil in the lives of the students, as committed and caring educators we must attempt and be willing to respond to their complex needs (Postman, 1995). There is a difference between transforming social ills and addressing social circumstances. When we seek to respond, we engage with students as collaborators in the process of change. We are capable of discovering resources, answers, and alternatives that bring hope to students.

This is exemplified by our response to the needs of homeless students and young parents. Recently, two of our homeless students, who were also pregnant, found themselves without health care and without support. One support staff member, Alex, spent days working with housing managers and other city contacts until the students were able to get an emergency placement and health center committed to provide ongoing prenatal care for them. Despite it all, the students are active learners, coming to class to complete their education.

Another area of learning for us was prompted by the evening child care situation. When half of one's students are young parents who depend on unreliable child care resources, an attendance and tardiness nightmare is inevitable. For the past two years, the academy has struggled to find day care at the school, but a school built in 1927 cannot provide the space and environment that young children need. This summer, two of us devoted substantial effort to working with two large day care providers to develop evening care slots. In the fall of 1997 we introduced evening care for the first time. As such programs work for us, we hope that other organizations will try them.

We have to understand as we engage with young students that our experiences and thought frames are not necessarily the norm for students today. As adults, we tend to prescribe and construct images, frames, and scripts (Goleman, 1985) and expect the students to respond to them and participate in them. Our learning at the academy is that many of these young people are reconstructing and renaming language that may have once had negative connotations (Goleman, 1985). The students' language becomes the mechanism for the construction of their reality, which is represented by language that is different from ours (Berger and Luchmann, 1966). For example, our wellness counselor, an African-American woman active in the civil rights movement, during student orientation last year had her students divided into groups discussing gender roles in society. A word commonly used by males, females, African-Americans, Hispanics, and Anglo-Europeans alike today is *nigger*. Students would say, "A girl only wants a nigger money," "a nigger wants his girl to give it up. . . ." The discussion went on for half an hour until the exasperated counselor exploded, explaining her experiences and the reason she and others had fought against the use of the word. One young African-American student replied, "Miss, we will respect you and will not use the word around you, but that's not what the word means to us. Can you understand that?" Over the next few weeks there was a lot of discussion among the staff about our imposition of frames and scripts upon the students. It prompted us to ask ourselves how open we are to students taking language that may have been oppressive to us and redeeming and reclaiming it to fit their scripts and frames. We have no answer yet, but we are having the discussion with students and in our staff meetings.

Alternative approaches to learning

In the latter 1970s and early 1980s chaos theory, together with influences in quantum physics, created a lasting impact on the organizational and scientific structures in the world. The assumption that small changes and insignificant deviations would not have any lasting effect on an environment was proved wrong (Gleick, 1987). The dichotomy between order and disorder, structure and chaos had been shattered. The early concepts and frames about predictability and control shifted.

This new insight brought forth new patterns of viewing the universe. We were to discover that within the chaos and disorder there is a source of order (Wheatley, 1992). Within the universe, factors are not independent but related; within chaos are boundaries and stages. These notions challenge us to break from the linear thought process of seeing things in separate states (Wheatley, 1992).

New ways of thinking

At the academy, this new way of thinking has forced us to view the circumstances of our students, their behavior, and their issues as small deviations that affect learning. In one case, we had a young student mom who was with her nine-month-old at the hospital, and so could not read for class or do other homework. The student's English teacher evaluated her situation and determined that her personal chaos and disorder could become an opportunity for creative learning and reflection. The young mother was asked to keep a log, to share her discovery about the growth process, to share about her experience at the hospital, and to discuss how to manage the situation as if she were speaking to others. We also learned from chaos theory to view the universe differently and, by integrating the everyday relationships of the student, to allow those circumstances to mediate the student's learning and stimulate the use of new thinking tools and skills. Within the disorder in the lives of the learners are patterns that can lead to new knowledge.

Chaos theory offered insight into the interrelatedness of the universe, stating that undergirding all interactions are relationships within systems. As educators at the academy, we have been challenged to find the relationships that exist outside the normal and rigid academic standards of the regular classroom environment. Nathan, for example, was a great student, but he wanted his contractor's license. He needed two math courses and an additional English course to graduate. We were able to provide only one math class. Nathan went to a local college. There he sought two college courses required for the contractor's license. He negotiated with the dean of the college and with the administration at the academy. He presented faculty at the academy with a course on contract estimation and one on framing and building. His English teacher agreed to give him an independent study regarding architecture in Boston. He read novels, books, magazine reviews, and articles about architecture in the city. He prepared a paper on the matter and also passed both of the two courses with an above-average grade. What we learned from Nathan was that he used his learning skills to think critically. He was able to examine a real-life scenario, one with many obstacles, and come up with viable options. Within the subject matter he read and researched, he was able to integrate theoretical knowledge with the practical realities of everyday life.

The greatest learning we are experiencing in our teaching is to look at the deterrent factors that affect students and their academic gaps and turn them into areas of self-development. The work of Peters (1987) has encouraged industrial leaders to reorder, rethink, and refocus on factors that historically have been interpreted as obstacles in the production and manufacturing process—and turn them into positives. The challenge for us from Peters' work was to reconceptualize these so-called deterrent conditions, viewing them not as feedback but as alternative contextual realities that need to be included and considered in any learning and management situation. This would require reengineering the educational delivery, production, and service process to use change, adversity, and chaos as creative elements in the design and development of a product, with full participation of all stakeholders in the organization.

We applied these ideas with students like Beatrice, who struggled most of her academic life with science. Last year Beatrice needed to select an area of science and health and write a major paper about it. She chose nutrition and exercise. Focusing her paper on the development of fat cells, she spent hours at the college library, visited hospitals, and spoke with a nutritionist. Her paper was a practical research guide for a young mother. She provided tips to parents on how to address the issue of chubby kids. In addition, she shared information about ethnic foods and diets that were culturally appropriate. This was a student mediocre in regular science to the point that she had failed science in prior years. The difference in her learning now was freedom, creativity, support, constant coaching, and the expectation that she could do this and be effective. Her area of greatest difficulty and so-called deficiency had thus become an opportunity for learning. We are reminded that these simple solutions and techniques are the "invisible obvious" (Farson, 1996, p. 25) that allow for creative transformational results in teaching and learning.

Exploring and experimenting with change

The metaphor of students as pioneers in an ecosystemic change process has substantially influenced the learning process at the Downtown Evening Academy. The role of leadership has been to create opportunities for faculty to discuss the realities of the students and the school. The staff and faculty have slowly begun to hear about new frameworks like those of Wheatley and Kellner-Rogers (1997), Goleman (1995), Covey, Merrill, and Merrill (1994), and Bennis and Townsend (1995). The process of learning and discovery has been supported through informal conversation and small discussion groups. In addition, everyone at the academy has opportunities to seek a response or explanation for any occurrence or obstacle encountered in the program. Two staff members have had experience working with small organizations and have used their prior knowledge to create an open dialogue. The major focus of all staff development has been on team building and open discussion.

We have been and are still "thriving on chaos." It is a chaos that has emerged from a context of change and reform in both academic and political structures in Massachusetts. As a pilot school, we have the flexibility to move away from the old way of doing things and seek to develop new venues for learning. We have been aware that traditional academics have failed to address students with alternative learning circumstances.

The academy has been struggling recently with shifts and changes, seeking to be proactive in its response to student needs. A major role of leadership is to assist in forging and developing a vision that can be owned by all staff. It is actually the art of mobilizing and organizing (Kouzes and Posner, 1995). The envisioning process entails seeing where the future lies and assisting other staff members in discovering and envisioning the possibilities. As a leader at the academy, my major role is to foster confidence through the demonstration of competency, caring, and profound commitment (Kouzes and Posner, 1995). As an instructional leader, my major role is to allow staff to discover and inductively relate their experiences to the ongoing change process. This process has required patience and openness to dialogue about why the unfolding vision is grounded in certain frameworks. Staff at the academy have slowly begun to understand and incorporate the frameworks in their professional practice. This has been demonstrated in their creativity around directed studies, their use of technology, and their eagerness to develop an alternative learning curriculum and environment.

We have also had to address political issues at the academy that affect the direction and development of the school. A major reality is that we are in a political environment that continually changes priorities, outcomes, and expectations. Our schools, programs, and focus must always take into consideration the political context of education. When a district lacks a mechanism for cutting through political red tape and other obstacles, then schools must establish other vehicles to influence the system as a whole. School communities need to be proactive, ready for any request, and ready for chaos. We must be willing to engage with the district in developing new paradigms for effective practices that will lead to addressing our students' needs. We must be able to seize the moment and lead our schools into a process of continuous renewal and improvement. Tomorrow starts today, and today is now.

References

Bennis, W., and Townsend, R. *Reinventing Leadership: Strategies to Empower the Organization.* New York: Morrow, 1995.

Berger, P., and Luchmann, T. *The Social Construction of Reality: The Sociology of Knowledge.* New York: Doubleday, 1966.

"Boston Graduates." *Boston Globe,* June 24, 1997, City Section, p. 1

Covey, S., Merrill, R. A., and Merrill, R. R. *First Things First.* New York: Fireside, 1994.

Farson, R. *Management of the Absurd: Paradoxes in Leadership.* New York: Touchstone, 1996.

Freire, P. *A Critical Encounter.* London: Routledge, 1994.

Gleick, J. *Chaos: Making a New Science.* New York: Viking, 1987.

Goleman, D. *Vital Lies, Simple Truths: The Psychology of Self Deception.* New York: Touchstone, 1985.

Goleman, D. *Emotional Intelligence.* New York: Bantam, 1995.

Kouzes, J. M., and Posner, B. Z. *The Leadership Challenge: How to Keep Getting Extraordinary Things Done in Organizations.* San Francisco: Jossey-Bass, 1995.

Peters, T. *Thriving on Chaos: Handbook for a Managerial Revolution.* New York: Knopf, 1987.

Postman, N. *The End of Education: Redefining the Value of School.* New York: Vintage Books, 1995.

Sikes, S. Presidential inaugural address at Bunker Hill Community College. Boston, Aug. 1989.

Wheatley, M. J. *Leadership and the New Science: Learning About Organization from an Orderly Universe.* San Francisco: Berrett-Koehler, 1992.

Wheatley, M. J., and Kellner-Rogers, M. *A Simpler Way.* San Francisco: Berrett-Koehler, 1997.

FERDINAND FUENTES *is director of the Downtown Evening Academy, an alternative pilot high school within the Boston Public School system. For the past ten years, he has worked with inner city youth and with prevention efforts in a number of diverse community organizations and educational institutions.*

*A native Indian educator shares a difficult story of change for
the children, faculty, and families in the Vancouver school district, where for many years native children were the least likely
to succeed and the most likely to be disciplined, labeled as having behavior problems, or recommended for alternative programs. Collective actions and strong leadership have resulted in
major improvements for all members of this school community.*

4

Aboriginal children: educating Canada's throw-aways

Lorna Williams

I REMEMBER THOSE FIRST few weeks in my new job as native Indian
consultant for the largest (in 1984) school district in the province
of British Columbia. I was hired to work with the district's two
thousand Aboriginal students.

These students are approximately 3 percent of the total student
population of fifty-seven thousand, but they comprise 40 percent
of those in behavior disordered classes and 20 percent of those in
communications classes. More than 50 percent of the Aboriginal
students of secondary school age are in alternative programs (usually off campus), which only go to grade ten. At that time, few aboriginal children graduated from secondary school with diplomas
that gave them future options. My position was established in
response to a critical report on the district's native Indian education services, which listed fifty-seven recommendations covering
curriculum, staffing, programs, and parent and community
involvement.

NEW DIRECTIONS FOR SCHOOL LEADERSHIP, NO. 6, WINTER 1997 © JOSSEY-BASS PUBLISHERS

One recommendation was to create a native advisory committee to advise the district in developing programs and services for native children and to raise additional funds. Another recommendation was to hire a coordinator of native ancestry. The district decided instead to hire a consultant who would belong to the teachers' union rather than be a coordinator at the management level. This effectively placed the position outside all decision-making opportunities. However, the district decided to break the provincial norm by placing the position not in the student services division with special education but in the program services division that managed curriculum implementation, program development, resource development and implementation, media and technology, race relations, French programs, and some English as a Second Language programs. This was very progressive because it gave the position access to subject specialists, resource selection, and professional and staff development. Although the position didn't fit on the district's hierarchical organization chart, over the years this ambiguity allowed me to develop programs and services by working with every employee group in the district. I was not bound by traditional organizational rules and practices.

The first five years I reported to the deputy superintendent, who was responsible for all education services at the district level. I could see there was fear in hiring a native Indian, due to our efforts to resolve our unjust treatment in Canada and our increasing demands for existing and outstanding Aboriginal rights. Also at issue was hiring a person of a specific ethnic heritage into a professional position. I was the only non-Caucasian at that level of the organization.

I met with the deputy superintendent every week or two for about two years, and I made sure I was on time or early because of the myth that Indians are always late. These meetings proved crucial in initiating, developing, and implementing programs. He supported me in many ways: as a mentor and a devil's advocate, he challenged and directed me to develop my ideas. He asked questions, we discussed articles and issues reported in the media, and, by attending every function that I planned for teachers and students, he demonstrated that native Indian education was a priority with the district. Even today people remark how good it made them feel to know he was willing to learn about education for native children. He gave personal feedback, through letters, regarding his knowledge of people's work. In a large bureaucracy it is important to acknowledge people's efforts.

Another realization that came early in my career with the district was that I had to confront my own fear of being fired and placing myself and my family at risk economically. Those of us who are hired to create a change for a specific population within an organization run the risk of making enemies and being resented for demanding that the organization change. Fear heightened my feelings of vulnerability, which made me at times indecisive. I had to "let the job go" in my mind in order to push the district to the extent needed to make the necessary changes. I kept myself focused on my work, which was to make positive educational changes for Aboriginal children. It was also important for the district administrators to see that I was respectful of their institution and wanted to work cooperatively with them.

During my initial interview, I asked what the district's vision was for native education. No one attempted to answer the question. Articulating the vision would be my responsibility. I knew that if I did little it would be acceptable, because no one knew what to do to change the failures native children were facing in the district. I also knew that the urban Aboriginal community would be watching me closely to see if I had "sold out" to the white establishment in order to be employed by them. Few knew my work because I had recently moved from my reserve (reservation, in the United States) and my teaching experience had been entirely in a band-operated school. Although there are differences between the rural and urban contexts, size and number of schools, and working with one First Nation only (as opposed to working in a district where the students were from many First Nations across the country), the knowledge I gained through life experiences and working in my community served me well in understanding the needs of children and their families. Another difference was the provincial jurisdiction of the city schools rather than the federal jurisdiction of the schools on reserves.

North Side School

My first week on the job I was invited to a meeting to discuss a program the district had opened two years before and moved from a secondary campus to an elementary campus. It was a program for students in kindergarten to grade nine, with a focus on native cultures. It was expected that the program would not cost the district any additional funds other than the basic education amount covering teachers' salaries and facilities. The cultural component was supposed to come from First Nations elders volunteering their time and wisdom, and from the staff who would modify the curriculum to infuse cultural content into the academic subjects. As I walked through the classes, I noticed there were very few books or other teaching materials; there were First Nations crafts such as leather work, beading, weaving, and wood for carving, but no maps or science equipment. I asked the teachers what texts they used to teach the academic subjects. They told me they used photocopies of workbooks they paid for from their own pockets. I asked them to list the textbooks and equipment they required.

There were problems with the design of the program, but the greater challenge was the negative attitude of the staff in the main school, even though that school had one of the highest populations of Aboriginal students (about 40 percent of the school). Moving the program in portable classrooms onto the campus added another sixty to eighty students. I was invited to meet with the staff on a professional day and would have two hours to try to help the staff understand Aboriginal children. I wasn't sure where to begin. I brought several maps of the First Nations territories and languages. I explained that in Canada there are ten language families, seven of them found in British Columbia, and that those seven families include thirty-four different languages, which in turn have many dialects. I wanted them to understand the backgrounds of their students.

One of the teachers asked, "Why is it that the natives in my class don't know which tribe they are from? I have to tell them. I know more about them and their history than they do." I explained that as the European settlers moved across the country the land was carved up in different ways: first by the trappers; then by Methodist, Anglican, and Roman Catholic missionaries who had the province divided amongst them before the middle of the nineteenth century; then by the federal government, which set the boundaries for reserves; and finally by the province, which joined the confederation in 1876 and expropriated many reserve lands. Aboriginal people were confined to smaller reserves, and often the names assigned to tribes had little to do with their nation names; frequently the people were divided into bands and put onto small portions of land.

I also explained that in Canada, Aboriginal people are deemed to be subjects of the federal government. Within the government and judicial system we are called Indians; in the media and otherwise in public we are called native Indians. Since 1980, Aboriginal people have been reestablishing the use of their proper nation names. Although the names coined by fur traders, explorers, government surveyors, anthropologists, and missionaries are still stubbornly used for individual tribes, the label "Aboriginal" is used when referring to the collective. The term Native Canadian has not gained popular use as Native American has in the United States, primarily because we have only recently been allowed to vote (1962 federally and 1956 provincially). Many parts of Canada have not formally negotiated a treaty or terms of governance with Canada. Therefore, many Aboriginal people will not consider themselves Canadians until there is a negotiated agreement about the terms of their relationship. So what that teacher thought he knew was probably not accurate.

There were other questions from the staff that afternoon that proved useful in articulating the issues that required addressing in

First Nations education: "Why are the natives so transient? They come to school for a few weeks and then they are gone. Sometimes they leave to return home for a funeral and they don't come back for three months." "Why don't the parents support their children's education?" "Why do natives let their children make important decisions, such as whether they'll attend school or not and when to go to bed? The kids come to school so tired they fall asleep at their desks." "Why are they so quiet?" "They come in late most mornings, and they never catch up. I've tried everything. I finally gave up, though I don't want to, but I have to think about my responsibility to the rest of the class." "Do you think it would be a good idea to schedule the recess and lunch breaks for the native program later than the main school? They are always starting fights on the playground." "Why is there a Native Indian Cultural Enrichment worker when there isn't one for the Chinese or Vietnamese? Their cultures are important too." "They come to school so unprepared. They don't know their alphabets. Some of them don't even know how to count, and they are in grade three. The psychologist says they are not learning disabled, they need one-to-one attention. They can learn when I sit with them, but I can't do that, it isn't fair to the other children." "I send notes home for the parents to come but they never show up. The support of the parents is important. Educational research says that the more parents are involved in the education of their children the more successful the child." "The native parents never show up at parent-teacher night. They even shut the door on the native worker when she visits them at home." "I'm so frustrated."

I tried to answer some of their questions, though the answers were inadequate. One asked, "What can you tell me or give me that I can use in my class on Monday morning? If you can't do that, this is a waste of time." As I was collecting my things to leave, a teacher said to me, "I just love them. That's the best thing, just love them."

The principal asked if I wanted my first tour of Vancouver School. It was an old, dark, bleak building with high ceilings and lots of windows. I noticed in the book room some maps and elementary textbooks. I asked him if the native program could use them if they were not being used. He said he'd ask the staff. Later he told me the staff didn't want them lent out because they might need them. I sat in my car in front of the school, feeling inadequate. I thought, "Maybe I don't know enough to help our children survive in an environment like that school. Surely someone else would know what to do." Fortunately, my family totally believed in me and my ability to do the job, and my rich experience as a member of the Lil'wat First Nation had prepared me more than adequately for this work.

Reflections on my own education

I remember my first day of school, skipping down the trail to keep up with my older brothers. They taught me some English words like "no," "yes, teacher," "my name is Lorna." My second older brother told me to watch the teacher's eyes if I wasn't sure which one to say. When her eyes got big, say yes. If they got hard and squinty, say no. That was a magical year. I learned to speak English, to read and to count. I remember answering questions for the grade twos, who were also in my class. Our teacher was firm, patient, and had a very kind face. I was eager to learn. The following year I was sent to residential school 150 miles away. I didn't know what was happening. I thought my whole family was going on a trip, but only an older sister and I got on the train. My father and mother were left on the station platform. I cried for two years and became incommunicative. At the end of the second year I came home with a broken foot and hepatitis, so the nurse and my parents decided that I would not return to the residential school. When I returned home, I had lost all language. I confused English, French (spoken by the nuns and priests), Shuswap, Chilicotin, and our own language, Lil'wat. No one understood me, so I stopped talking altogether.

As an alternative to residential school, I was sent to a Federal Day school close to home. It was just as horrible. I was in a constant state of confusion, fear, and loneliness. The teacher made me turn my desk around to face the corner, because I couldn't read and I couldn't remember what she had just taught the class. She knew how to humiliate us and took every opportunity to punish us. My brothers had a difficult time learning English; they often forgot themselves when they were talking to their friends, naturally returning to our language. I remember hearing the swishing of the teacher's skirts as she rushed down the aisle to smack one of my brothers across the head or to hit another child with her ruler. Once she pulled a boy's ear so hard she tore it. After that incident some mothers began a campaign to get rid of her. Before then no one had told their parents what she had done.

Education the Lil'wat way

Among the Aboriginal people, much of the training and education of the young depended on the close relationships formed and fostered by the entire family. During the infancy stage the elders in the community and family spent the most time with the infants, talking to them, caring for them, anticipating their needs so that they didn't need to demand to be cared for. A child was very seldom out of sight or left alone. Everyone intensely observed each child to gain an understanding of their gifts and the qualities of each child's personality. Supporting the development and realization of those gifts, as well as bringing forth from the child qualities to help each one achieve a balanced personality, demanded intense observation by the elders. At five or six years of age the children were given over to the older siblings so they could play and work with them. In this way, strong attachments were made with older children, and they learned to be responsible for others. They had to learn patience and to teach younger children. As children entered puberty, they were encouraged to spend more time with aunts or uncles, who became the primary teachers. Later, youths would choose their own teachers. If they were interested in learning how to do a particular thing they would find someone in the community proficient in it and approach that person. They negotiated and mutually agreed on how the studies would take place. This often meant moving in with that expert's family. As I was growing up, many young men and women lived with us for a time while working with my parents, and sometimes my younger siblings and I lived with our aunt and uncle or with our older siblings. In this way we learned to be independent while still part of a group, and we also learned to be competent on the land.

Decolonization of education

In 1967 the federal government presented a white paper in Parliament proposing to demolish Indian reserves. It argued that the reserve system was the source of social illnesses and that full integration into Canadian society would solve the problem. But in 1973 the National Indian Brotherhood responded with the document "Indian Control of Indian Education," which outlined the direct involvement of Indian parents in the way their children would be educated and in local control of education. The paper was accepted by the government as national policy. Since 1973, 454 band-controlled schools have opened in Canada. They are now important sources for new materials in literature, social studies, First Nations languages, and innovative programs. Until then such decisions were made by an Indian agent on behalf of the federal government. This policy finally brought the opportunity for meaningful engagement in education by the First Nations parents and community.

A school for two worlds

In 1969 in my community of Mount Currie, nine grade six students, who were to be bused to the neighboring white community to continue their schooling because the federal government was closing classes on the reserve, told their parents that they were quitting school. They said they would not attend the public school because "kids who went to that school had to fight and were made to feel stupid and failed anyway." The parents had no choice but to find a way to educate their children at home. The implementation of the National Indian Brotherhood's policy paper on education enabled Mount Currie to be the second community-controlled school to open in Canada. The community articulated two goals for the new school: to hire teachers from our community and to teach our language and tell our own history. We had two qualified teachers in our community, which meant we needed a teacher training program to train other community members.

The local school board negotiated with a young and progressive university to design an off-campus teacher training program. A community-based teacher training program was necessary for five reasons:

First, to train teachers to focus on the educational needs of our community. It was felt that the general university training programs did not adequately prepare teachers to teach Indian students, hence so many failures in the public school system. We had to devote our studies to find out why our children failed in their academic studies. Was it the instructional methods used? Was the curriculum alienating because our history was negatively presented? Was it the impact of colonization and oppression or the differences in world view and philosophy?

Second, to meet the goal of reviving and retaining the Lil'wat language. This meant that we needed to develop the Lil'wat orthography, describe the grammar, and develop a writing system to teach in school. Learning through literature is today's norm, but until recently our language and history were passed on to the next generations orally. Some of our younger teachers in training were not fluent Lil'wat speakers and so had to learn the language in order to teach it and use it in their classes. A 1972 survey found that the majority of community members age thirty-five and older were fluent, but the percentage decreased in younger people. However, a few children who lived with their grandparents came to school with limited English fluency.

Third, to design a system that educates community members for life on our land. They need preparation for employment and a satisfying life in our community, as leaving is an option very few choose. At the time, few had graduated high school, and the majority had fewer than eight grades of education, so we needed to provide educational opportunities for all members of the community. My sister, one of the two teachers in our community, taught pensioners how to read and write; she recalls their excitement as they learned to sign their government pension cheques at the bank.

Fourth, to understand and envision how a community can survive in a cash-based economy, with limited accessible resources left on the land, a diminished land base, and the constant threat to our aboriginal rights. This means understanding the impact on our lives of municipal, provincial, federal, and international government decisions and laws.

Fifth, to understand how to coexist while maintaining our right to our own identities and way of life. We wanted our children to be educated such that they could move freely within and between different worlds without compromising their identities as Lil'wat. We needed to understand how our families had changed due to forced removal to residential schools and to separation of families into single-family dwellings. And we needed to grapple with the effects of family violence and abuse of alcohol. I was fortunate to witness and participate in community traditional activities before they were submerged by social breakdown, so I knew that social breakdown was not our normal way of relating in our world. Our school had to focus on how to construct a new social system based on combining traditional and current ways.

The university helped us by finding instructors to come to our community to teach what we needed to learn. It allowed us to interview and select the professors and to negotiate the course content and the methods of evaluation. Some people at the university felt we would negotiate for leaner and easier courses, but the professors who came consistently reported that they had to work very hard to meet our demands and that they had met no students who worked harder than we did. It took us longer to complete our studies—ten years, on average—because all the teacher trainees had families with young children, we worked at the school full time, and we were active in our community's life. We studied a broad range of disciplines such as linguistics, psychology, sociology, anthropology, English, political science, history, and education. From the teachers in training our community needed classroom teachers, administrators, curriculum developers, language majors, adult educators, and preschool and early childhood teachers.

We searched the world to understand our reality. We studied the work of Bronfenbrenner to get a picture of how new societies like the Soviet Union and Israel had dealt with working mothers' children. We studied Franz Fanon (1963) and Paolo Freire (1970) to understand how a colonized and oppressed people must challenge the way they have been socialized to see themselves as inferior. We studied the methods used by Cuba to reverse a 90 percent illiteracy rate. We learned to be critical of the literature on native learners written in Canada and the United States, where they were described as passive, silent, lacking in motivation, undisciplined, underachievers, noncompetitive, lacking goals, apathetic and unengaged parents, truant, and erratic school attenders who had different learning styles. Many researchers cited cultural difference as the reason for lack of school success. The underlying thinking was that our cultures were inferior to modern western culture because we were an illiterate culture without organized societies. Our low level on the verbal scores on English language tests was attributed to native cultures being 'silent,' ignoring native children's consistently high scores on the comprehension components of those same tests. The researchers failed to realize that knowledge had been transmitted orally throughout our histories through a complex system of stories and ceremonies. My uncle, for example, knew by memory the boundaries of every family's territory, including all the changes due to deaths and births. People respected him for his accuracy and fairness, relying on his memory to settle conflicts or disagreements about ownership. My family and community were not silent. However, we differ in how we use language and in our interaction patterns. Children are encouraged to ask questions until puberty and then are discouraged from asking questions of adults.

In 1979 I came across some articles by Reuven Feuerstein, an Israeli teacher and psychologist. At first I resisted and became angry at what he had to say, because he spoke of cultural deprivation and cognitive deficiencies. I was tired of being accused of being deprived and deficient because of my culture and ethnic background. However, I kept going back to it and realized that the work of this man was exactly what we were searching for all these years. It was relevant for many reasons. He worked with children and youth who had become separated from their families, communities, histories, and languages, who were traumatized over a long period of time, or who had not been to school until adolescence—children who survived by not trusting adults. He also spoke of the social, cognitive, and emotional effects of deprivation of one's own culture. He argued that every society establishes adequate and effective educational processes to prepare their children for the future, and that knowing your past is important to finding your way in the challenges of change and adaptation. Some of his ideas that I found particularly striking are the following:

1. All children can learn to learn at demanding and abstract levels.
2. Tests must reveal the procedures and strategies that a learner is using, rather than the learner being penalized and judged by a test's unfamiliar content.
3. Teachers are part of a collaborative relationship with learners and must see themselves as learners too.
4. Teachers and examiners must be willing to adapt to their relationship with the learner and be willing to convey to the learner that what the student is being taught is meaningful and important to the teacher too.
5. Teachers must be willing to share the power and control in the classroom and to take every opportunity to invite students' knowledge and life experiences into discussions (Feuerstein, 1980).

Connecting what is learned in the classroom to life outside it is a powerful way to teach students to transfer knowledge from one context to another. If we don't validate students' knowledge, in time they disregard and distrust the knowledge they acquire through their life experiences and feel that school learning is not relevant to them.

Feuerstein also created structured applications to actualize his ideas: a cognitive curriculum with instruments, a teaching process called mediated teaching, and a dynamic assessment called the learning propensity assessment device (Feuerstein and others, 1983) that can be administered individually or in a group. What I learned from Feuerstein and others in my years of study served as a framework for understanding education in a larger context, which helped me design and implement programs and services for one school district.

The urban context

I read all the files and the literature left behind by my predecessors, and I met with all employee groups who came into contact with students of First Nations ancestry. The principals reported their frustration at the mobility and transiency of the students; many said that they registered fifty to eighty such students in September and at the end of June had a completely new set of fifty to eighty. Typically, students reaching grade four had been in four to seven schools. Their records rarely kept up with them; through the years it is easy to lose files and, for that matter, the student. The principals reported little cooperation from parents and complained that native students taxed their time, energy, and resources in a way unfair to the other students.

The district required more culturally sensitive programs. Counselors reported that the type of school counseling they were contracted to provide was not what the students required, and they asked if I could find a way to arrange the necessary counseling. Teacher librarians asked for guidelines for selecting resources and publications to add to their collections, but when I provided a workshop on bias and discrimination in learning resources using examples from their collections, they hotly defended the right to freedom of speech and noncensorship. Many teachers didn't want to hear the history of First Nations in Canada, claiming that time is past, they didn't have anything to do with historical wrongs, and so they shouldn't be made to pay for their ancestors' actions.

I asked students why so many of them dropped out of school. They cited many reasons: racism, prejudice of the teachers and other students, drugs and alcohol abuse by older members of the family, family violence, the need to look after siblings, moving around too much (in the city and back and forth to their home communities), peer pressure to hang out and skip classes, and teenage women having babies with no one to help them. (In 1994 we counted thirty-five young women with children who wanted to complete their schooling.)

Parents said the school lied to them about their children's progress. Reports and discussions with the teachers led them to believe their children were doing well, but in some cases students were not able to read in grade seven; the parents didn't find out until enrollment in grade eight, when a counselor would explain that the school didn't have the appropriate services for their children. Parents didn't want their children to be sent to a segregated program, they wanted them to receive the necessary support in their neighborhood school. The parents' mistrust of native alternative schools was the result of the continued failure of their children in those programs.

I met people at all levels of the district who were searching for ways to help Aboriginal students. Jim Cummins's article "The Empowerment of Minority Students" (1986) provided me with a framework to build the services, programs, and strategies. He explained that the power relationship in society is reflected in the school and classroom. The broad areas for intervention necessary to change the school achievement levels for Aboriginal students were the following:

- Changing the attitudes of all district personnel away from devaluing Aboriginal people and toward valuing their history, languages, cultures, beliefs, and world view

- Increasing parental engagement in making educational decisions for their children and increasing their understanding of the public school system
- Shifting the focus of assessment from legitimizing disabilities to enabling professionals to enhance and direct instructional practices to support student learning
- Providing students with opportunities to gain a positive sense of their First Nations identity and to change their negative belief of themselves as learners
- Addressing the complex language issues, including acquisition of academic school language as well as an understanding and appreciation of language usage in the students' home and community; offering First Nations language classes in the district is a long-term goal.

Language

The speech language pathologists (SLPs) were particularly receptive to working with me. I had no idea what they did, how they assessed, or what they did with the information they accumulated on a child, so I asked the SLP at North Side school if I could follow her for a few days. I met other SLPs, and we began to plan some workshops and language development projects in some schools. We offered a summer language development program in a nearby First Nations community that ran for more than three years. It involved children from ages four to twelve and their parents. We continued the program in the school over the year, and a teacher-consultant worked with the school staff to assist them in understanding the language differences of the students, as well as coaching them to increase the children's response rate in the classroom.

Another project was to assist the teachers to understand the ways questions are used in an Aboriginal home. Even if the language spoken at home is English, excessive questioning is discouraged, reminiscent of traditional social rules. Asking questions of students to which the teacher knows the answer is annoying and irritating to them and can cause them to become silent. Aboriginal students also need more time to think about a question before answering than is usually allotted in classrooms. At the same time students need to know the rules that govern the participation structure of a class, so we need to teach those directly. Other programs that have proved to be highly beneficial in addressing the language needs of students are Feuerstein's Instrumental Enrichment, a structured and highly interactive cognitive education program; cooperative learning; and Maria Clay's reading recovery program, an intensive program for five- and six–year-olds.

Assessment

School psychologists helped me understand their role in the district. I met one who studied with Feuerstein and who wrote a master's thesis on the shortcomings of the standardized assessments when used with Aboriginal students. With her support, I applied for a grant to train thirty-five school psychologists, speech language pathologists, special education assistants, and teachers in Feuerstein's Instrumental Enrichment training in the use of dynamic assessment, in particular the learning potential/propensity assessment device. Except for two who could not see its benefit, the members of this group became the core unit of staff who expanded the program throughout the district. In the course evaluation they said what they valued most was realizing that they had given up on students far too quickly in the past. They were excited that they could learn so much about the child's learning habits and that they had the tools to help a child learn more efficiently. Another benefit was the shift they made in discussing a child's assessment, especially the engagement of the teachers in the discussion. This was of great importance to me because in many cases the teachers' voice was not as strong as those of the other members of the school-based team even though the teacher is the pivot between assessment and intervention. Also, the focus of the discussion was on the child's learning, the efforts it will take to make a positive change in a child's approach to a task; the type of teaching required to help a child transfer what was learned from one context to another; and what the child was able to master with mediation from the assessor.

This group initiated monthly network meetings to discuss specific cases to have the benefit of the group's insights, to discuss reporting issues, to plan future training sessions, and to review and extend their understanding of Feuerstein's structural cognitive modifiability theory and other complementary theories. We have organized annual training sessions in dynamic assessment over the past eight years. Every September the school psychologist, speech language pathologist, and teacher (occasionally the counselor) of certain elementary and secondary special education classes administer the group dynamic tests. These have been extremely beneficial in directing the assessment goals for the school and in helping the teacher know where to concentrate her efforts in class instruction.

Staff and professional development

In-service training and workshops were given to extend people's knowledge, understanding, and appreciation of First Nations. These were a few of the workshops:

- A six-day drum-making course in which the participants learn about the significance of the drum and its use in First Nations. In addition to constructing the drum, they learn the different songs and drumming styles from across the country, compose their own songs, and create a design from their own significant life experiences to paint onto their drum. The instructors weave stories and songs into every lesson. Teachers have changed their music, art, and socials studies curriculum as a result of the course.
- A workshop to help teachers modify subjects such as science to

include First Nations point of view.

- A display in the district board room on the uses of every part of the cedar tree, open to all staff in the district office. Comments in the evaluations said they appreciated learning about all the uses of this familiar resource, and they were surprised by the scope and depth of technical knowledge achieved by Aboriginal people.
- Workshops on the use of story telling in traditional education.

Another stream of courses was offered on understanding the effects of forced assimilation, colonization, and oppression. These included an intensive week-long simulation experience on topics such as racism and biased attitudes toward women, homosexuals, immigrants, refugees, Aboriginal people, and people with disabilities; classes about issues between Canada and First Nations, self-government, land claims, and determining resource conservation and exploitation; and conferences involving indigenous people from around the world to stress our common experiences.

Curriculum resources and staffing

Over the past dozen years we screened curriculum materials for bias and relevance, made every resource available to teachers, and searched for and recommended purchasing replacements. We developed new materials as well as worked with publishers and filmmakers to produce materials. I worked with all human resources officers to seek and solicit applicants of First Nations ancestry and to modify the officers' established interview and selection practice to take into consideration cultural differences. Through use of Canada's human rights policies, we have advertised and hired staff for designated First Nations programs and services to increase the Aboriginal staff. Since 1984 we have increased the native teaching staff from three to twenty and support staff from seven to forty-five. The next challenge is to increase Aboriginal staff in every part of the district.

Parent and community involvement

It has taken an enormous effort to convince school staff that Aboriginal parents want the same thing for their children as any other parents: a good education that will enable them to be full participating members of their communities. I realized that the two groups were afraid of each other and relayed this message to both groups. As the schools made attempts to involve parents in meetings and school events, a pattern emerged. Some parents or community members at school meetings would become angry and verbally abusive, which in turn caused the staff to pull back, hurt and upset. I met with the staff to explain that they needed to hear the parents out and give them an opportunity to describe all the pain they had experienced in schools. It was the first chance Aboriginal parents had to say these things to anyone in the education community. I urged the staff not to take it personally but to simply listen.

Each school's approach to engaging parent and community participation has been different, but they have similar elements: they are focused on student learning; they acknowledge that parents want to know what their children are learning, especially about new technology; and they involve parents in planning school events and give them a space in the school that they feel is theirs. The parents seem to understand that even though education was used against them, it is still important to their children's future.

The First Nations Education Advisory Committee has among its members representatives from district staff, trustees, First Nations services and programs, teachers' unions, administration, district parents, and First Nations community organizations. Through the committee's work the urban Aboriginal community has a vehicle for input to and direction of Aboriginal education in the district.

Since 1984 there have been times I felt like giving up; coincidentally, at each low point colleagues, students, and parents encouraged me by showing me that my efforts have made a difference in their lives. This work has been rewarding in many ways. It has challenged me to take what I learned in my life and translate it into programs and services. I've had opportunities to grow professionally and personally. I have become more clear about the importance of the articulation of one's cultural identity and understanding how one's life experiences affect everything we do. I have also come to a greater appreciation for the complex role of teachers in society, and after twenty-five years of teaching children and adults, I find this profession continues to be stimulating and invigorating. My passion to advocate for children whom society deems disposable remains the motivation that guides my work. The elders in my community, in traditional times, regarded children as gifts to the community and thought that as adults it is our responsibility to draw out those gifts and find a place in the community for every child.

References

Cummins, J. "The Empowerment of Minority Students: A Theoretical Framework." *Harvard Educational Review*, 1986, 56(1), 18–36.

Fanon, F. *The Wretched of the Earth.* New York: Grove Press, 1963.

Freire, P. *Pedagogy of the Oppressed.* New York: Seabury, 1970.

Feuerstein, R. *Instrumental Enrichment.* Glenview, Ill.: Scott, Foresman, 1980.

Feuerstein, R., and others. "Learning Potential Assessment Device." Unpublished manual, Hadassah-Wizo Institute, Jerusalem, 1983.

LORNA WILLIAMS, *a Lil'wat from Mount Currie, B.C., is a teacher and consultant for the Vancouver School District No. 39, a position she has held since 1984. She is the author of Lil'wat language curricula, children's books, and teacher's guides. She codirected the video series* First Nations Circle Unbroken *and was the associate producer, narrator, and consultant on the internationally award–winning documentary* The Mind of a Child.

The author discusses the effects on students of teacher expectations, ethical role modeling, and shared leadership, demonstrating how these practices contribute to a safe, healthy, and achievement-oriented school culture.

5

What you expect is what you get

Karen Moore

I BEGAN MY PRACTICE OF TEACHING in a medium-security prison. Not exactly the environment that a teaching school would prepare one for. That I had not come from a teacher preparatory program didn't seem to matter to the administrator who hired me. Apparently, he hadn't received many applications from candidates with teaching credentials. My supervisor later told me that my nightclub management experience was evidence to him that I could handle a potentially rough crowd and that experience was more important to him than my lack of teaching credentials.

From the beginning, I decided that the inmates I was to teach would become my students, period. No other labels seemed necessary or appropriate for the job I was trying to do. This attempt to bring some humanity to an inhumane and oppressive environment is what I would point to as the main reason for much of the success I had while working "behind the wall." My classes were filled with young men, most of whom came from impoverished backgrounds, who in the past had been labeled anything but students. The other labels they had been given or had involuntarily taken on validated them in ways that a wimp label like "student"

NEW DIRECTIONS FOR SCHOOL LEADERSHIP, NO. 6, WINTER 1997 © JOSSEY-BASS PUBLISHERS

never could. Why then did they take so readily to being renamed as students now? Perhaps the brutality of prison life provided them with a reason to want to make changes in their lives and in how they thought of themselves. As their teacher, I learned my first important lessons: that my power was directly related to their power, and that my students would live up to my high expectations of them if I respected them as learners. What you expect is what you get. I expected my students to be committed to improving themselves and increasing their knowledge and skills. That's what I got. So began my career of working with and empowering students whom others called by different names.

In college, I had been introduced to the work of the Brazilian educator Paulo Freire. Freire's notion of the process of education as one of dialogue between teacher and student has had a profound impact on me and on my teaching practice. The most important elements of true dialogue, according to Freire (1970, pp. 76–81, my emphases) are "*love*, a profound love for the world and for men; *humility; faith*, intense faith in man, faith in his power to make and remake, to create and recreate, faith in his vocation to be more fully human; *hope* and *critical thinking*, thinking which perceives reality as process, as transformation, rather than as a static entity." The power inherent in Freire's philosophy became very evident to me in my work with students. I continually saw the effects on my students of renaming and relabeling, both in prison and in the school that I now direct. Teacher expectations are where it all begins.

In 1987, Rosenthal wrote about the "Pygmalion Effect," in which researchers studied the effects of teacher expectations on student achievement. The results, put simply, are my working thesis: *what you expect is what you get*. Although this may sound simplistic, the negative proofs are evident in almost every school system in this country. Whether we call students underachievers, unteachable, nonacademics, unruly, discipline problems, bad students, or potential dropouts, *what you expect is what you will get*. The powers of naming, classifying, and labeling are awesome and should never be taken lightly by educators. Teachers and schools help students define who they are by what is expected of them.

As Perrone (1991, p. 33) has observed,

Moreover, and possibly more important, life in classrooms is shaped by the expectations that are held for children. No matter how good a school might appear physically or how many books and computers exist, if teachers don't believe firmly that *all* children can learn and *all* children have important interests, intentions, and strengths that need to be seen as starting points for ongoing learning, they are failing children, their families, and their communities. And when children are seen as failures or deemed not capable of full participation in the best that schools provide, their educational possibilities are stunted. I have been in too many of these schools.

LMACS: *a different kind of school*

Since 1991, I have been working at the Lowell Middlesex Academy Charter School (LMACS) in Lowell, Massachusetts, with what I like to call "school leavers," otherwise known as high school dropouts. The one thing I have found that school leavers have in common is that at some point in their young lives they have somehow acquired negative labels. Many have been given these labels in their homes, and they come to school already "damaged." What teachers then do with these students either can help them change or can reinforce those negative labels. Over the years, I have watched students live up to the names and expectations that others, specifically school personnel, have given them. I have worked with other educators to develop strategies that raise the expectations we have for our students.

Many of the school leavers I work with are what Herbert Kohl calls *non-learners*. I believe that these students have resorted to nonlearning as a response to families, school curriculum, teachers, and communities that have disrespected them as students and as learners. I have usually found nonlearners to be of above-average intelligence, an intelligence that is not reflected in their school grades, most of which are at C level or below.

Kohl's conclusion (1991, pp. 10–11) is much the same as mine, as I continue to see incredibly bright young people who have lost their zest for learning:

Learning how to not-learn is an intellectual and social challenge; sometimes you have to work very hard at it. It consists of an active, often ingenious, willful rejection of even the most compassionate and well-designed teaching. It subverts attempts at redemption as much as it rejects learning in the first place. It was through insight into my own not-learning that I began to understand the inner world of students who chose to not-learn what I wanted to teach. Over the years I've come to side with them in their refusal to be molded by a hostile society and have come to look upon not-learning as positive and healthy in many situations.

For many of my school leavers, leaving school was, in fact, a very positive move. While in school, they were relegated to the lowest tracks (a practice that many schools refuse to acknowledge still occurs), according to either their past performance, ethnic background, or economic status. The students' negative school histories followed them like a shadow throughout the school system, never to be challenged or removed. Upon coming to our school, these school leavers find that all bets are off, so to speak. Beginning with the initial interview, it is made known to them and their families that in our school they are starting fresh, and we have very high academic expectations for them. How high are our expectations? College preparatory course work is the standard. All students must take college entrance examinations to prove competency in English reading, writing, and mathematics before they are allowed to graduate. This standard is for all students, with no exceptions. Regardless of their past performance or academic history, all students are expected to be college ready before graduating. Getting them ready is the special challenge of some extremely dedicated, hard-working, cutting-edge teachers with whom I am proud to work.

In 1995, we were granted one of Massachusetts's first charters to open a public school. Until then, the school had been operating as a partnership between the local school district and Middlesex Community College. Upon receiving our charter, we set about designing a school-based management structure that would form the infrastructure for our school for former high school dropouts. Our school is located on the Middlesex Community College campus and serves one hundred students, ages fifteen to twenty-one. The school-based management team consists of four full-time teacher-counselors, two counselor-teachers, the assistant director, and the director (me). Although the challenges to starting up a school have been myriad, I would like to focus on the reason for our being a school in the first place and how our high expectations, shared leadership, and ethical role modeling address the school's biggest challenge: our students, who have already demonstrated that they are school leavers (dropouts).

Teacher expectations

One thing all of our students have in common is having acquired negative labels. By the time they come to our school, they are all, at minimum, high school dropouts—a powerful negative label. Many also bear other negative labels. One young man in particular comes to mind. He had been expelled from his previous school for stabbing another young man with a pair of scissors. His name was Jim Doobey and, according to his record, he would not make a model student. During the initial interview, in which all students are required to participate, he disclosed that his father had recently passed away. It was evident from his voice and the tears in his eyes that he missed his father quite a lot. One thing I try to do with all of our students is to make them feel special for the good things that they have done, are doing, or may do. During Jim's interview, in a moment of inspiration, I decided to label this young man our Good Doobie. A good doobie means someone who goes above and beyond the expected behavior, with an almost annoying predilection toward being good. He laughed when I told him what I was going to call him, and at that moment it was hard to see the violent young man that his record showed.

In our weekly Thursday meetings, the entire staff goes over any concerns we have about students, and we share pertinent student information. At our next meeting, I relayed to the staff that we had a new student who was going to be our Good Doobie, in spite of what he had done to be expelled from his last school. The staff members all laughed, some of them nervously, and I learned later that a few used his new name when they came into contact with him. Call it coincidental, but our Good Doobie became just that: an honest-to-goodness Good Doobie, the kind of student that any school or classroom would love to have. Every time a teacher called him our Good Doobie, Jim would smile sheepishly. During the time he spent with us, it became evident that he had been stuck in the anger part of the grief process, and his violent acting out had been a terrible response to his lack of control over his loss and his inability to change the way things were in his life.

His very negative behavior produced predictable responses from his former school community, which actually encouraged him to continue acting out. Our different reaction to his "record" produced different results. Throughout his time with us Jim continued to work on his anger management skills while acting out the part of our Good Doobie.

Today, Jim has graduated and is now a member of the Marines. I hope he will keep the Good Doobie label that we gave him. *All teachers, especially those working with adolescents, have a profound impact on how students define themselves.* This impact happens in every teacher-student encounter, both verbal and nonverbal. I commend the staff at our school for trusting me in what sometimes must appear to be my capricious attitude toward how I ask people to think or treat certain students. When working with adolescents, I have found that unpredictable responses can work wonders toward changing old thought and behavior patterns. Many of our students need to learn how to trust adults whom they expect to act in very

predictable ways. I like to give our toughest students some surprises, good surprises like positive names, increased responsibilities, and requests for their opinions on school issues. What you
expect is what you get.

Shared leadership

At our school, we have attempted to build in times for a collegial
sharing of practice, curriculum, problems, and accomplishments.
Every Thursday, we meet for an hour solely to discuss student
issues. Initially, these meetings tended to digress into complaints
about students, until a member of the counseling staff reined us in
and reminded us that we had to also highlight our student successes. Now a part of our meetings is the ritual of reminding each
other of our success stories. On Fridays, we have staff meetings to
take care of the business of the school. Policy decisions begin and
end here. Only after the staff has identified an issue or policy does
it go to our board of trustees for approval. The Friday agenda
always includes "other business"; after two years, staff members
have input into every aspect of how the school is run. As the school
director, sometimes I gauge how well I am doing by how comfortable my staff is with disagreeing with me and taking on leadership
roles themselves. Using that gauge, I'm doing very well.

The implementation of school-based management at our school
means that all constituencies are heard from before any policy decisions are made. Although this style can be cumbersome, I have
found that staff participation in every decision that affects the
school creates a climate of openness and trust, which I believe is
necessary for a healthy school. Modeling the behavior and attitude
that I want from my staff is the way I get it. Many times, I believe
that my greatest asset as a school leader is my ability to be quiet and
listen. Although I often believe I know the best solution to a given
problem, I have found that unless the staff is in agreement, it ultimately doesn't matter what I believe. The downside to this
approach is that occasionally my reticence creates the appearance

of a power vacuum, which some staff members may rush to fill. When this happens, I assert my commitment to valuing everyone's ideas by asking whoever hasn't been participating in the conversation for his or her opinion. This invariably reconnects the entire staff to the issue at hand. Decision making at our school is a matter of who gets to make what decisions and when.

This model of shared leadership works in our school. Trust building among educators is a slow process. There generally exists a climate of mistrust between teachers and administrators that goes beyond individuals and has to do with roles and positions. Unfortunately, it is part of our current education system. What you expect is what you get. After two years, our team has progressed to the point where we can disagree with each other and still come to some creative, complex solutions to our issues. We have come to understand that consensus decision making doesn't necessarily mean that we all agree on everything.

The creative tension ever present in our school also necessitates ongoing, systematic professional development to address our high risk of burnout. On any given Friday, we may be debating the implementation of our suspension and expulsion policies (rarely used but much debated), planning next semester's team teaching opportunities and course descriptions (which are constantly changing), planning the monthly ethical value assembly (where everyone participates in skits, readings, songs, and active examples of the ethical value for the month), reporting on updated rubrics and curriculum changes (which are never-ending and sometimes exhausting).

Our model of shared leadership also works with our students. LMACS has very few school rules, and those that we do have must make sense and be agreed upon by everyone affected, including students. In my opinion, one key to working with adolescents is avoiding conflict—that is, taking away many of the unnecessary rules and regulations that they seem particularly inclined to break or get around. This rule breaking is a developmentally appropriate activity, and we have found that adolescents need to have very few, but strong and sensible, parameters to feel secure. These are our rules: all students must come to school, do their work, get along with others, abstain from all forms of violence and substance abuse, and try their best to fulfill their graduation requirements in the most timely manner.

Ethical role modeling

As a school, we have come to rely on our ethical values to ensure that the unspoken curriculum of safety, respect, and responsibility comes across loud and clear. We also actively teach ethical values. The thematic curriculum we use with our students focuses on the ten ethical values that students in our first-year ethics class identified as being the most important for us to teach and learn. In addition, the adult members of our school community believe that their own daily behavior affects the interactions and relationships among the students themselves—and, ultimately, the school as a whole. How else would we teach ethical values but by modeling them daily for our students? Although this may sound simple, it is far from it. The process of doing this takes much time, shared reflection, and a willingness to act and react differently than we are used to—three qualities that are usually in short supply in schools.

The combined effect of teaching ethical principles while modeling ethical behavior is profound. Although at many times in their past our students have acted in violent, disruptive, and antisocial ways, we have never had a violent incident in our school, and disruptive episodes are rare. It is simply not a part of our school culture to act and react in ways that have become "normal" for many schools. *If administrators and teachers want to change student behavior and attitudes, they should start by modifying their own behavior and attitudes.* Students learn to act in the ways we have taught them to act. What you expect is what you get.

Here is an example of the way this axiom works in our school community. While I was driving two Hispanic male students home from the end-of-year student-versus-staff softball game (where the students outscored us two to one), one of the young men turned to me and said, "You know, Ms. Moore, most of the students at LMACS had a lot of trouble with teachers in our other schools, acting disrespectful and you know. Now if any of you ask us to do anything or to stop doing anything, we do it immediately. No questions, no problems. I think that's because all of you showed us respect *first*, and now we can respect you."

At our school the adults, through their behavior, show students the meaning of such abstract terms as respect, responsibility, truthfulness, and courage. We work daily to create an environment in which we can all be comfortable teaching and learning. Utilizing Freire's model, our lives have become the curriculum. How we manage the school directly contributes to our lack of problems. The students learn much more from watching how we act and interact than they learn from what we have them read, write, or do. Although this type of ethical behavior and shared leadership does take a lot of time in the beginning, ultimately, the time that many schools take going over the same old unsolvable problems becomes unnecessary.

Critical ingredients: one interested adult . . . and a compelling mission

At the Harvard Graduate School of Education's Risk and Prevention Program, where I studied resiliency in students, the most important factor preventing students from failing or leaving school was identified as *one interested adult*. Quite simply, the research shows that the strongest protective factor against school failure is the existence in a child's life of a single adult who has taken a personal interest in that student. Unfortunately, many students have not yet encountered that one interested adult. Why is this? How can it be possible for a young person to go through school and not encounter one adult who is personally interested in him or her?

Large classes and large schools make such personal encounters difficult if not impossible. I have yet to hear of a teachers' collective bargaining organization negotiating the dismantling of a large school or even negotiating for smaller classes. Perhaps if teachers' organizations decided to concentrate on these proven strategies to make schools better, they would have more success in their endeavors and more support from their communities.

Our school has no collective bargaining organization, and I don't believe that the teachers feel at all disenfranchised. Instead, they now have become active participants in the school management, which provides them with a bargaining tool that is far stronger than what they ever had before. The collegial trust that has been developed among all of the school staff has contributed to a highly professional school organization. Our mission is to ensure the success of our students. I believe that a school's mission can only be accomplished if all adult members of the school community agree on how to daily implement that mission. At our school, if it means we need longer school hours to accommodate our students' lives, we extend the schedule. If it means a varied course load with teachers working in multiple subject areas, they work to achieve that. If it means that we must hire additional personnel to provide the scaffolding of skills necessary to achieve our high standards, we rearrange the budget to accommodate those personnel changes. A whole school dedicated to reform means that everyone is actively involved. No one has ever complained about working too much, and the teachers generally work nine-hour days. Our mission is what drives each of us to expend the extra effort if it becomes necessary. We are dedicated to getting the job done no matter what it takes. This is how the professionals work at our school. *What you expect is what you get.*

References

Freire, P. *Pedagogy of the Oppressed.* New York: Seabury, 1970.
Kohl, H. *I Won't Learn from You!* Minneapolis, Minn.: Milkweed Editions, 1991.

Perrone, V. *A Letter to Teachers.* San Francisco: Jossey-Bass, 1991.
Rosenthal, R. "Pygmalion Effects: Existence, Magnitude, and Social Importance." *Educational Research,* 1987, *16*(9).

KAREN MOORE, *founder and executive director of the Lowell Middlesex Academy Charter School, received her master's degree from the Risk and Prevention Program of the Harvard University Graduate School of Education. She is a member of the National Middle College High School Principals Consortium and has been working with at-risk youths since 1988.*

The keys to improving the success rate of throw-away children
are the appropriate intervention and timing of educational
strategies.

6

The boy who hid

Myra Chang Thompson

In any environment any one can be successful if he or
she has the right supports.

Nancy Mather

DANIEL'S CASE IS A STORY OF SUCCESS. After years of reading failure, he participated in a public school program where teachers
identified areas of need and provided appropriate instruction and
support. Daniel's foremost tasks were to improve his reading skills
and emotional reactions to difficulties. He could make little
progress until he could view himself as having these skills. A
school-based team approach, a student support group that encouraged self-advocacy, specific learning and teaching strategies, and
building on a personal interest made Daniel's success possible.

Early problems

Daniel was conceived by his sixteen-year-old mother and unnamed
teenage father. Information about the mother is sketchy. Daniel
may have inherited a severe learning disability from one or both of
his biological parents. The exact date his mother decided that she
could not care for him and gave him up for adoption is not known.

NEW DIRECTIONS FOR SCHOOL LEADERSHIP, NO. 6, WINTER 1997 © JOSSEY-BASS PUBLISHERS

Lee Ann and Tom Parsons were a young professional couple. Tom was an English teacher at a local high school. Lee Ann studied music and was both a professional pianist and teacher. They had a young daughter, Catherine, but were unable to have more children. Tom suggested that they look into adopting a second child, and Lee Ann agreed. Within a year, an infant boy was available for adoption.

Daniel came to live with the Parsons when he was six days old. The couple's comfortable ranch home was perfect for the young family. Catherine took to Daniel immediately; she loved having a little brother. Lee Ann and Tom's families were delighted with the addition. It looked like a perfect picture.

But Lee Ann, a young and sensitive woman, began noticing subtle things about Daniel. Almost immediately he needed to be held all of the time. He seemed to need to know that his new family was at hand. He was of average size and weight but was a difficult eater. Lee Ann remembered how difficult it had been to establish routines and schedules. Daniel did not fuss or cry—he appeared withdrawn. The family doctor recommended changing Daniel's eating formula and prescribed extra vitamins. The family was adjusting to Daniel, but Tom thought Daniel was depressed. Could infants be depressed? Could Daniel have been aware of his real mother abandoning him?

Daniel began to gain weight and grow as time went by. He had two sets of doting grandparents who visited regularly. Love and affection were lavished on both children, but Daniel responded differently than had Catherine at that age. Lee Ann felt that Daniel was extremely sensitive and insecure. Both parents noticed that Daniel reached various developmental milestones much later than Catherine had. He was slow to walk and talk. When he was older, he would run away when he was scolded. One day when Daniel was about two-and-a-half years old, he grabbed a spoon out of his sister's hand. Lee Ann spoke firmly to him, telling him he needed to ask his sister for the spoon. Daniel burst into tears, ran out of the room, crawled under his bed, and refused to come out. When Tom came home later, he found Lee Ann and Catherine lying on the floor trying to coax Daniel out; Tom joined them and eventually Daniel emerged. Several other episodes occurred, each ending with Daniel hiding under his bed with his face to the wall.

Gradually Daniel began to understand and accept that the Parsons were his family. He learned to trust them and they, in turn, demonstrated in a concrete way that they were there to support him. Their bond deepened. Tom and Lee Ann began to understand that Daniel was a special boy. Catherine, without being told, kept an eye on Daniel in the neighborhood when he played. He, like his sister, was accepted by the other children.

As Daniel grew and became more communicative and active, the family noticed other subtleties. When Daniel was given verbal information, it took him a noticeable amount of time to respond. His language patterns were unusual; Lee Ann described them as mixed up. It was as though he had the words he wanted to speak, but they were spoken in a different order. Also, Daniel's balance was poor; he fell and ran into things frequently. Then Lee Ann began to notice a new behavior: Daniel was becoming increasingly stubborn. Once he began a task, such as eating, he could not be hurried into finishing or trying something unfamiliar. The family doctor was again consulted and assured Tom and Lee Ann that Daniel's growth was within the average range of development, though his language was atypical. Tom and Lee Ann worked to make their life and family as normal as possible. They reassured Daniel that they loved him, and they let him know that he was all right.

Daniel appeared to outgrow many of his early childhood problems. His coordination and language skills improved. Daniel had many good language models to provide stimulation and practice, including Catherine, a verbal and bright child who included Daniel in many of her activities. Her friends were his friends.

Learning problems

Daniel was enrolled in school when he was six. The first few years were fairly uneventful except for Daniel's difficulty learning to read. Arithmetic skills were quickly and easily mastered by Daniel, though he had difficulty remembering the letter names, sounds, and words he was taught. He became easily frustrated with processes that seemed totally alien to him and would stubbornly refuse to try. At home, he occasionally burst into tears. He tried hard, but reading was an immense chore. His parents continued to support him and read to him regularly.

Socially, Daniel was a charming and entertaining young boy. He was good-looking and kind to other children. He spoke in a slow and deliberate manner, but he was always understood and in return understood everything that was said to him. But he could not understand why he could not read and why it seemed so easy to other children. At the end of second grade, he was recommended for retention. His parents were quite disappointed, but they knew Daniel's progress in reading had been minimal at best.

The second grade teacher also recommended that he be evaluated to identify the reason for his reading difficulty. Daniel was told about the evaluation by his teacher and parents. He wanted to know why he could not read but was unable to bring himself to ask the adults who tested him. Suddenly he began to realize the small but growing feeling that something about him was not right—maybe he was stupid or retarded. He just knew that when it was time to pick up a book and read it, it might as well have been written in a foreign language. Maybe, he thought, that was why his mother had given him up for adoption; maybe she knew something was wrong with him.

Actually, the assessments indicated that he had above-average intellectual ability but a moderate-to-severe learning disability. Lee Ann and Tom did not quite understand the findings but agreed that Daniel should receive additional reading help. Daniel then received special education services in reading and spelling when he repeated grade two.

Onward to special education

Now that Tom and Lee Ann had a child in special education, they felt they had to view things differently. They continued to read to Daniel and to involve him in Scouts, organized sports, and other children's activities. But they steered away from asking Daniel to

read. They did not want the situation to get any worse. Their
hearts broke for their son; they feared the joys of literature would
never be experienced by Daniel in the same way they had experienced them. They still loved and cared for Daniel, but their expectations changed.

Daniel made little progress in reading over the years. Different
programs were tried and abandoned. Daniel became so anxious
about reading that it was uncomfortable for the teacher and other
students. Still, he was encouraged to do what he could. He liked
having other students read with him. In his way, he did continue to
try. But reading was so laborious and slow that he often forgot what
the sentence said by the time he got to the end, and he'd have to
start over again. He was very good at answering the comprehension questions, but reading was quite difficult for him. Daniel found
ways to creatively get out of reading or to guide the discussion to
extremes so that there was no time to continue the reading. He was
clever and charming, and though his tricks did not always work, he
learned how to avoid as much as possible this task that he so dis-
liked. Reading was not only difficult for him, it made him feel inadequate. It was one of the few things he could not do well.

Daniel was, for example, a very good math student, although
Catherine often had to explain word problems to him. Science and
social studies were also of great interest to Daniel until the reading
assignment was made. Homework assignments that involved reading could be completed with the assistance of his family, but class
assignments were another matter. It was one thing to struggle with
reading in the resource room, but it was totally humiliating to be
asked to read in the classroom. The seconds ticked loudly from the
clock on the wall as Daniel waited for a giant hole to open up and
swallow him, saving him from having to read. Until the teacher
told them to stop, other students in the class whispered the words
to him in an attempt to get him through the dreaded torture.

Daniel was devastated every time this happened. He had
no way to deal with it, sank lower and lower, and was sure something serious was wrong with him. He felt bad. He could talk with
no one. He felt bad. He tried so hard, yet nothing came. He

felt bad. His friends and classmates did not understand either. He felt bad.

He had to feel better.

Along the way Daniel developed new strategies to deal with his crippling performance in reading. He never volunteered to read. When he was asked to do so, classmates would groan, knowing that his attempts would be long and unproductive, and eventually the teacher rarely asked. Daniel used his charm and imagination whenever possible to get out of reading too. And it worked.

Small successes

In the resource room with the special education teacher Daniel could relax a bit. He knew she was not going to push him very hard. One day the resource room teacher had Daniel open a box. In it was another new reading program to try. Daniel rolled his eyes. She seemed very cheerful about the program. It was written for problem readers and contained high-interest material with stimulating pictures of topics of interest to boys. Daniel surprised himself by picking up the books and looking through them. He was very interested in the book on sports and borrowed it to take home that night.

The book was a small paperback with a colorful cover and illustrations. He read the cover. He opened the book to the first page. There was one sentence on every page. He slowly began to read the book. He knew some of the words. He made up words he thought would make sense if he did not know the real words. He read every single page. It took him two and half hours to read the book—the first complete book he'd ever read by himself! He was exhausted from his concentrated effort. He was happy, for awhile.

But Daniel was rapidly approaching adolescence, and it hit him hard. All of his feelings of failure seemed to pile one on top of the other. He confided only in Catherine. Not only was he still grappling with being abandoned, adopted, and feeling out of control, he felt that he must be retarded. He began to doubt the love of his parents. He pushed them away. Catherine ran interference. Daniel struggled to contain his outbursts but could not manage them. He screamed at both parents for no apparent reason. He frequently left the room in a huff and slammed his bedroom door behind him. He was irritable and bad-tempered. He argued loudly about topics that earlier would have been minor.

The entire family was knocked off balance by the sudden change in Daniel's temperament. Tom spoke with a counselor at school, and together they decided Daniel might benefit from individual counseling if the situation did not improve. The counselor suggested ways to improve the communication between Daniel and Tom and to set limits before the entire family became upset. Tom and Lee Ann talked over the situation and decided that individual and family counseling would be a positive way to work out some of the problems. They would need Daniel's cooperation. Slowly the family adjusted.

Grades seven and eight were difficult for Daniel. His classmates no longer cared to support him. They voiced his suspicions when they called out, "Retard." It cut him to the quick, and Daniel quickly adopted new strategies to help him cope with this new level of stress. He was well spoken, nicely attired, from a good family, and had a wealth of experiences in his background. He learned to be aloof and became smart in math, oral discussions, and other areas in which he had ability. Developing all of these qualities, however, did not prepare him to deal with the problem he thought was obvious—that he was retarded.

Daniel did not communicate his personal difficulties to his parents or family. Catherine began college when Daniel was in eighth grade. He missed her, but she came home frequently, and they retained their closeness. He had this disability that was as clear as the nose on his face, yet despite his doubts a new awareness emerged: maybe he was not completely retarded if he could earn passing grades in math, play sports, and discuss ideas with his father! Yet he questioned everything, including his parents' love.

Summer had always been Daniel's favorite time of the year. There was no school, he was allowed to stay up late and sleep in late, and his sister was home from college. Even though Catherine had a summer job, she included Daniel in many of her activities. The summer before entering high school was especially fun; his parents gave him more freedom and treated him as a grown-up. His baseball team came in second place in the championships, and he had four close friends who saw each other daily, got along well, and suffered in common from the awkwardness of being a young teen. They began to notice girls at about the same time, and they were all sad to see the summer end. Two of the boys would attend the high school across town, and the remaining two would attend Lawrence High School with Daniel.

Lee Ann was taken aback by how mature Daniel looked. He was nervous about the first day of school and did not hear a single thing his mother said. He worried about getting lost, entering the wrong class, or being hazed by a senior. Catherine had taken him to the school, shown him around, and told him about the teachers; they walked through every building even though she knew it was unlikely he'd have classes in all of them. Tom went over the schedule with Daniel but knew it would cause problems because Daniel frequently reversed numbers and letters—finding the classrooms might be troublesome. Tom did not want to make the problem bigger by drilling away at it and simply suggested that if Daniel needed help, he could ask a teacher.

Daniel walked through the hallways to his homeroom. Mr. Brand thrust out a big hand and shook Daniel's, welcoming him to the class and telling him to sit anywhere. The students received books, reviewed class and school rules, and were given the first week's worth of homework assignments. This was not so bad, Daniel thought to himself.

Daniel dreaded only one class: special education. He was scheduled to receive special education assistance in reading, writing, and spelling instead of enrolling in English. He surveyed the hall and quickly ducked into the class. What he found were students, some from his former junior high school, of all grade levels and two adults, a teacher and her assistant teacher. The students introduced themselves and talked briefly about the year and their expectations. The teacher presented each member of the class with a contract, which had to be read and signed by their parents. She would also sign it. The contract said that students would work their hardest to do their best and to be responsible, and that the teacher would do the same. The group was cooperative, and Daniel thought it did not sound too bad. It was different than his previous special education classes.

The school year began quickly. Daniel tried out and earned a spot on the ninth-grade football team; he dragged himself to school every day after a physically tiring practice and finishing late-night homework. Every night there was math, science, and social studies homework. The math was not much of a problem, but the science and social studies always involved reading and written work. He was not thrilled about it, but he complied. His special education teacher joked with him and assigned him to work with a student who was a stronger reader but not so good in oral discussions. "Maybe you can help each other," she suggested. She also began a discussion group in which he and his classmate learned to speak to each other about their disabilities. They were hesitant at first, but slowly the histories of pain, failure, and frustration were revealed.

Daniel would not accept help from his parents. He did not want them to know how poorly he read. If they saw his written work they would insist on him correcting it. It was easier if he got through it by himself. When the first marking period ended and his grades went home, Daniel was surprised. His parents accepted that his grades were just passing. Daniel knew he could do better, and thought that school might not be so bad after all.

Academic improvement

By the time Daniel's annual progress meeting took place, the Parsons noticed a change in him. They reported that he felt less negative and anxious about school and seemed to be more willing to try some new things. The special education teacher suggested administering a new test to more accurately identify Daniel's learning problems. The Parsons agreed and met the teacher again later to discuss the test results. The new evaluation was able to identify strengths and weaknesses of Daniel's learning profile. Daniel scored well in reasoning and visually presented tasks. He scored poorly in auditory processing skills and in the ability to analyze and synthesize what is heard, which is necessary in early reading skills. An additional area of weakness was visual motor skills, where the eyes and hands are used together, such as when copying from the chalkboard, or where material needs to be completed quickly, such as when working under a time limit. Intellectually, Daniel continued to score within the average range. The psychologist noted there were emotional indicators or signs of emotional problems that were emerging. Each professional and parent left the meeting with a better understanding of Daniel's needs and how best to meet them.

A collaborative service plan

The special education teacher used the test results to determine Daniel's greatest areas of need. Reading, writing, and spelling skills were weak. Daniel's attitude toward reading tasks was also a target for change. He was recommended to a support group for this purpose. The teacher chose selected assignments in reading, writing, and spelling that were appropriate to his interest and skill level. As with all of the other students, when Daniel mastered a skill he was required to demonstrate it in an inconspicuous way. The teacher explained that this would help him feel more positive about his learning and build his confidence.

All of Daniel's teachers were asked to provide instruction using a visual component, a written outline, vocabulary words on the chalkboard, and a review of the material covered at the end of each day. Teachers also checked in regularly with the special education teacher to monitor progress and to try to emphasize common skills, habits, and strategies.

They all noted an improvement in Daniel's grades and his new confidence in carrying out classroom tasks. Mr. Brand reported that Daniel volunteered to read a paragraph in class on a regular basis. Regular tests were read orally for the entire class.

At the end of every school year the special education teacher offered students an option. Because there were two resource room teachers available, they could choose to remain in the same class next year or transfer to the other teacher, with no questions asked. Daniel chose to remain.

Tenth grade began with Daniel on the junior varsity football team. He still had the positive attitude from the spring. He had begun to notice the girls noticing him. After football practice there was homework and now phone calls to and from girls. The school curriculum remained unchanged: English, math, science, and social studies. Daniel signed up early for Mr. Brand's social studies class.

The special education staff carefully designed Daniel's program for the year. Reading, writing, and spelling skills were still the primary focus, but they would be imbedded in curriculum that was enticing and relevant to teenage learners. The discussions and support group for disabilities continued as part of the program. Materials were purchased that stressed life skills, everyday vocabulary, work-related skills, and study skills. A word processing program was acquired to assist with the writing skills process and Daniel's weakness in visual motor skills. Printed copies looked better than the students' handwriting. Students were given the choice to type their written assignment for other classes once they completed their work. The plan was to enlist Daniel's cooperation to complete assignments and practice sessions that he perceived as difficult.

Epilogue

Daniel's educational plan included confidence-building activities that allowed him to take risks in new learning situations. Activities were selected that allowed him to demonstrate his competence while building self-esteem. The school staff provided meaningful learning materials and activities that would make sense to him so that he was motivated to learn.

Behavior management techniques, including student-identified motivators, were used. Peer support, peer tutoring, and peer discussions were also in place. A system of self-advocacy was introduced and practiced. The teachers provided challenging activities when Daniel was ready to accept them. Classroom teachers also taught to Daniel's visual strength, eliminated time limits, and read tests orally to the entire class. By using road maps and other concrete means, they were able to get Daniel to focus on what needed to be accomplished and how it could be done.

Lee Ann and Tom's roles as loving and accepting parents were critical to Daniel's success. Many parents would have given up on a child like Daniel; their unwavering love and concern for him was the constant in his life.

Reference

Mather, N. "Alternative Strategies for Reading and Writing Instruction in the Classroom." Workshop for Massachusetts Council for Learning Disabilities, Concord, Mass., Oct. 1995.

MYRA CHANG THOMPSON *holds an M.A. in special education, learning disabilities from the University of Northern Colorado. She works as a special education consultant in charter schools and works with and trains new teachers in inclusion and individual learning styles.*

In Mott Middle College High School, educators and students are co-researchers in documenting the best practices in this high school designed to reengage the disengaged student. A caring approach with a focus on evidence of learning was the process modeled by the faculty and staff to shape the successful outcomes from this six-year-old institution.

7

Engaging the disengaged

Chery S. Wagonlander

ARE THERE IMPORTANT LESSONS that we as educators might learn about successful student engagement, disengagement, and reengagement from students and teachers learning together in a high school program specifically designed to be a safe haven for the disengaged adolescent?

I firmly believe the answer is yes. Through practical experience and careful research, our staff at Mott Middle College (MMC) has gained valuable insights into how to develop a learning environment that provides educationally fragile students with the support necessary to experience what has now become the school's motto: *a fresh start toward a successful future.* MMC is a ninth-through twelfth-grade public high school located on the campus of Mott Community College in Flint, Michigan. It has recently

NEW DIRECTIONS FOR SCHOOL LEADERSHIP, NO. 6, WINTER 1997 © JOSSEY-BASS PUBLISHERS

completed its sixth year as a county-wide, K–12/higher education collaborative that serves more than twenty-six public school districts in and around Genesee County. As a dropout prevention speciality school, its primary focus is to serve these districts as they work toward lowering persistently high dropout rates.

How many educators have the opportunity to create a "best school"? For how many is it coupled with the complete support of district, county, and higher-education administrators and dozens of key community members? And how many educators have this opportunity more than once in their career? I have had the good fortune twice: first as one of the founding educators of the Valley School in Flint, and second when I was hired seven years ago as the planner and school principal for a county-wide school reform effort to design and open the first middle college in Michigan. Both of these opportunities focused on creating new schools to meet the educational needs of students in the best way possible. Both turned into dream jobs from which I have been able to study the complicated process of student engagement.

In the early 1970s, the impetus for the development and opening of the Valley School was the first major teacher strike in Flint, which left many students out of school for a long time. Parents, already unsatisfied with public education, were pushed over the line and organized the first independent school in Genesee County. I became involved and remained at the Valley School for seventeen years as a teacher, counselor, and assistant headmaster. During those years, I became alarmingly aware of students who did not perceive themselves as fitting in at their home schools. Many students came to Valley because their parents selected the program for its excellence in education; however, a significant number and their parents were seeking a new educational environment in which healing—academically, socially, and emotionally—could take place. As a postgraduate student, I became more and more uneasy about America's continuing dropout rates. My growing concern coincided with a major effort regarding this problem that took place within the educational leadership of Genesee County during the 1989–90 school year.

Student disengagement: Longstanding problem, serious consequences

The future of a nation depends on the success of its youth. The implications of this statement now pose grave challenges to the world's political leaders, policy makers, and educators. Young people who fail to develop the basic skills and knowledge necessary to live as effective adults threaten us all. More specifically, American youth who fail to complete the first stage of their intellectual development by completing high school or its equivalent face a future of insecurity and limited opportunity. Lacking the skills and knowledge of a good high school education, they find themselves locked out of economic independence. Without tools and credentialing that a high school education provides, now virtually mandatory for meaningful employment, these youth are unable to take care of themselves or their loved ones. They are also ill prepared and thus unable to make substantial contributions to society.

In the late 1980s, college and K–12 administrators in Genesee County were wrestling with these issues, because they were committed to lowering longstanding dropout percentages in their districts and to increasing the number of nontraditional students going on to successfully complete a college education. After an exhaustive national search and analysis of programs designed to lower dropout rates, a three-way collaborative blossomed among the county's twenty-one public school district superintendents, the Genesee Intermediate School District, and Mott Community College. This collaborative aimed at blending the best components from research, school reform, and educational practice into strategies that would successfully reengage—and maintain engagement—of high-school-age students.

Reasons for disengagement

Research on the dropout phenomenon has identified multiple reasons students drop out of school before completing their high school graduation requirements. The reasons may be categorized into three broad areas, as shown in Table 7.1.

Problems related to life and family circumstances, individual personal problems, and school-related problems are patterns verified by multiple researchers. Students disengaging because of school-related issues is a serious problem that continues to call for creative interventions.

How Mott meets the need

By the 1990–91 school year, eleven middle colleges existed across the United States. These high school programs were all K–12/higher education collaboratives designed to lower dropout rates, increase the number of nontraditional students successfully enter-

Table 7.1. Reasons for student disengagement.

Life/Family	Personal	School Based
Low socioeconomic level	Legal problems	History of grade retention
Nontraditional structure	Learning disabilities	History of high family school delinquency
Lack of parent high school completion	Teenage sex and/or pregnancy issues	Course failures
African-American or Hispanic ethnicity	Substance abuse problems	Low grade point average
Unstable home life	Student's lack of internal locus of control	Truancy, suspensions and behavioral infractions
Trauma from divorce or death in family	Mental/physical health problems	Feelings of alienation from school authorities
Primary language non-English	Low self-esteem	Ability grouping

ing higher education, and reform the American high school. Each was modeled after the first middle college opened in 1974 at LaGuardia Community College (Lieberman, 1986). During the same year, MMC was created by more than 350 volunteers, including K–12 educators, college administrators, counselors and instructors, community leaders, parents, and students.

As planner of Mott Middle College, I have had the honor of facilitating the planning and then implementing and maintaining the middle college program. The group had the professional privilege of being entrusted with literally a blank slate for creating MMC by collaborating institutions, administrators, and their boards of trustees. This is a very important element in the entire process of successful school reform, for out of the directive to create the best, we educators were not told what to do or not to do; instead, we were given (and continue to be given) the protection, support, and respect necessary for total restructuring.

Beliefs that affected planning

From the beginning, we focused on designing a school that would deliver "intensive care" education by professionals sensitive to the school-related issues that, as we learned from research, caused students to drop out of school. It made sense to create a new school, with the goal that the learning environment would be the absolute best. The organization of the school and the delivery and assessment of instruction would need a successful blending of research and practical experience. It also became apparent that, if we as a planning group were to know to what extent our decisions regarding selection of best practices were quality decisions, data collection would need to take place from day one, and emphasis would need to be placed on quantitative and qualitative program evaluation.

MMC's special components

A guidance-based approach to all school experiences, with a heavy emphasis on the preparation of students for both the world of work and higher education, was developed. To accomplish this goal, real-world work and college course experiences are the sequence of study, and course requirements at MMC and all staff are expected to function as teachers and quasi-counselors.

MMC's program is centered around several key philosophical, theoretical, and research-based components with significant pedagogical implications:

1. Creating an environment of leaders and learners (Barth, 1990)
2. Applying "control theory-reality therapy" and "quality school" principles (Glasser, 1986)
3. Using "discipline with dignity" for student behavior problems (Curwin and Mendler, 1988)
4. Basing student assessment on "master learning" principles (Guskey, 1985)
5. Modeling "moral leadership" values (Sergiovanni, 1992)
6. Developing an "invitational learning environment" (Purkey and Nowak, 1984)
7. Planning curriculum centered on the five "dimensions of Learning" (Marzano and others, 1992)

MMC is grounded in a set of belief statements, a mission statement, and guiding principles of learning that are revisited annually for revision by the staff and school improvement team members. The core values that support our school's goals are reflected in our shared belief statements and guiding principles:

1. Schools are capable of improving themselves.
2. Educators have a responsibility to create, within the school, visions of good education.
3. Everyone who works in a school is not only entitled to a unique personal vision of the way he or she would like the schools to become but has an obligation to uncover, discover, and rediscover what that vision is and contribute it to the betterment of the school community.
4. All students can learn the school curriculum; some just need more time or a different approach.
5. Success breeds success.

6. Teaching is both an art and a science.
7. Educational decisions should be research based.
8. The school itself controls the conditions that ensure successful learning, and the school cannot evade the responsibility for establishing those conditions.
9. Curriculum should be aligned in relation to objectives, assessment, and materials.
10. Students benefit most from mastery-learning based instruction.
11. Students are responsible for their own learning, and teachers are responsible for creating a quality-with-equity learning environment.
12. Student outcomes should drive the educational system.
13. All people have the right to be treated with dignity.
14. All members of the school community are responsible for positive role modeling and seeking quality performance.
15. All people are entitled to live, work, and learn in a safe and orderly environment.

Best practice and professional experience

Foundational to the design of MMC are the findings from research on best practice combined with what the MMC staff has learned through the art and practice of teaching. The MMC staff developed and continues to refine a set of guiding ideas called "principles of learning," which are embedded in daily school procedures and teaching strategies. The major principles are an emphasis on the active role of the learner, a focus on learning that is relevant to learners, stressing increased academic learning time, recognizing the importance of self-directed learning, incorporating informal learning, emphasizing the application of content learning, providing role modeling of reflective behaviors, encouraging risk taking in an environment of trust and respect, providing regular feedback, stressing self-assessment of projects and progress, talking quality and expecting high performance, and recognizing that much learning takes place beyond the classroom.

This educational model is what we hoped would give MMC students the support they need to stay in school—and succeed.

However, it did not make sense that high school students who had already accumulated a disastrous GPA could truly have a "fresh start toward a successful future" if they were tagged for life with their old GPAs, even if all of our carefully planned elements were working smoothly. A few moments of simple mathematics will tell any educator that it takes three years of all A's and B's to pull an end-of-the-freshman-year .5 GPA up to a graduating GPA of 2.5. How many competitive college doors open with a 2.5 GPA?

Considering such information, the founding MMC staff joined me in creating a graduating scale upon which we wipe or adjust each new student's GPA to set in motion the observable goal of graduating with a 2.0 or higher. For many of our "want-to-turn-around" students, this practice allows them to meet the requirements of an incomplete, repeat a course, or take another course in the same core area. Also, we concentrated on developing multiple opportunities for "success connections" with MMC programs and the adults who run the programs. We view these decisions as necessary if we are expecting academically or emotionally fragile students to successfully develop new habits, attitudes, skills, and knowledge. Old patterns of failure, low self-esteem, and alienation needed to be replaced.

MMC students reengage

MMC has begun the tedious and intellectually challenging process of analyzing data collected over the last six years by teachers, administrators, counselors, and support staff. In addition to the data collected for program evaluation use, my doctoral dissertation focused on the first two classes to graduate from MMC. Teachers and students served as coresearchers. We are beginning to see some revealing patterns and themes in the research as we struggle to better understand the processes of student engagement, disengagement, and reengagement. A significant number of students do successfully turn around while attending MMC.

MMC statistics indicate growth

MMC's annual dropout rates (0, 2.2, 3, 6.5, 5 and 6 percent in six years, respectively) have remained lower than Genesee County's rate of 8.4 percent. MMC students' academic achievement has increased as indicated by both the Michigan Educational Achievement Proficiencies and the High School Proficiency Tests. Higher yearly scores also indicate a lessening of the female-male gender gap in both science and math and an increase in the number of students who receive state graduation diploma endorsements. Graduate follow-up surveys indicated that 74 percent of MMC's 1994 graduates, 64 percent of its 1995 graduates, 66 percent of the 1996 graduates, and 74 percent of the 1997 graduates are attending college, with 62 percent of all four classes attending Mott Community College. Ninety percent of all 1994 and 1995 MMC graduates reported they were working part- or full-time, with many combining attending college or raising children, or both, with work responsibilities.

MMC's fresh start, a college environment, the demonstrated belief in students' academic and personal potentials, different expectations, and the opportunity to change emerged as common themes during in-depth interviews with MMC graduates. Their follow-up surveys are filled with reports of success, pride, and improved self-esteem. Quantitative data concludes that many MMC students reached their goal of not only graduating from high school but doing so with dignity and purpose. Graduates' in-depth interviews emphasize the happiness that resulted from being treated like adults, being encouraged to make decisions and take new risks, and being given learning experiences that were fun, intellectually challenging, relevant, and group oriented.

Recurring themes

During their arrival and early years at MMC, students perceive many of the obstacles to their past school success as having been outside their control (such as unsafe schools, family problems, multiple moves, teachers not liking them, and the like), resulting in an important recurring theme of victimization. Also, a theme of alienation permeated 82 percent of student interview responses at the time of application to MMC, expressing feelings of separation, not fitting in, being different, not having friends, not belonging, and similar feelings. Analogous to the high percentage of victim statements relating to school factors, 66 percent of the students' comments expressing alienation connected to school-related factors: teacher-related behaviors, teacher attitudes, and teacher expectations or beliefs. A third major theme of boredom (27 percent of responses analyzed) emphasized that the students found work too easy and school boring. This boredom was a major obstacle to students' academic success. Only 8 percent of the responses indicated students perceiving their own socializing and poor attendance as obstacles to their success in school.

Most important, in addition to boredom being school related, most of the victimization and alienation responses were school related: teacher behaviors, student-teacher relationships, and classroom instruction.

Follow-up graduate interviews and ongoing MMC research offer insights into a student's movement from disengagement to engagement and how powerful the student-school "success connection," based on mutual positive attitudes and behaviors, becomes.

Reengagement: a deeper understanding

How did these MMC students, who three years ago were laden with heavy emotional burdens, poor academic records, and low self-esteem, mature into such positive and productively functioning young adults?

Quantitative and qualitative data analyses reveal a process common to many students who successfully reengage in school. Katlyn, for example, had been out of school for three months following multiple suspensions for fights with peers at school, insubordination with teachers, and truancy. She was angry at the world. She carried herself with a stiff body and a ready tongue. Easily triggered, Katlyn was determined to pick an argument before the day ended. Katlyn's mom wanted a warmer, happier future for her.

During one of her interviews, Katlyn focused on feelings of not being cared about: "Nobody cared. My mom cared. But nobody at school cared. . . . They didn't care what I did. It seemed like up to the eighth grade I had a 3.5 GPA. In high school, my grades dropped to .05 or something. I felt that nobody cared. . . . I just hated it. I used to fight all the time. All I used to care about was which 'skip party' I was going to go to. I missed three months of school."

Over three years, Katlyn learned to judge people and situations less quickly, to count to twenty and walk around the first-floor wing of the office area before speaking her mind, and to facilitate her younger sister's entrance into the MMC program. Katlyn is the mother figure for her sister and uses her acquired "control theory/reality therapy" principles when supervising her. She works full-time, takes one class at her local community college, and will be getting married in a few months. She openly brags about improving from a .5 GPA to an overall 3.5 GPA while attending MMC.

In these young people, the negative themes of alienation, isolation, failure, fear, anger, boredom, and depression were gradually replaced by such positive themes as empowerment and freedom, love and belonging, success, independence, and happiness. MMC graduates changed dramatically from their time of admission to MMC and their graduation. Isolation from the learning environment was replaced by proactive involvement in finishing requirements and acquiring a higher education. Katlyn remembered her years at MMC:

Because I could start over, I could erase the past: my grades, my attitudes, how I felt about myself. No D's or E's really had an impact on me. . . . You have to try harder for an A, B, or C. I make college friends; they helped me out a lot. It was fun. Learning was different. We got to learn different languages, doing learning instead of book reports. I remember the Health Seminar and getting to study. They [teachers] don't just teach you; you interact with your learning here. . . . If there had been no MMC, I would have been a statistic.

In-depth interviews with 1994 and 1995 MMC graduates indicated 88 percent were working, 81 percent were attending college, and 56 percent were juggling both. Twenty-eight percent were parents of young children. Forty-five percent of the students reported living independent of their families. Analysis of in-depth interview data identified several common themes and a shared pattern of the reengagement process describing a dramatic story of change, renewal, and self-discovery.

Data collected over a six-year period depicts a process of evolution shared by student after student. In this evolution, obstacles disappear and personal or academic failure are replaced by a time of discovery, change, and self-growth. This period then moves into a more stable phase in which new behaviors demonstrating positive academic and personal accomplishments are solidified. A large number of MMC students moved out of the downward cycle of school disengagement and disenchantment into a slow upward progression that included acceptance of both academic and affective knowledge about themselves, the development of positive teaching-learning relationships, and the exercise of behaviors focused on student choice, empowerment, recognition, and maturation. Three phases to successful student reengagement appear to possess common themes and behaviors:

Disengagement—depression, anger, dependency, alienation, boredom, presentism, self-focus, and apathy

Change-Maturation—confusion, suspicion, guarded openness, risk taking, limited trust, nervousness, questioning, limited involvement, adapting to change, hope, and excitement

Reengagement—belonging, tolerance, acceptance, giving, renewal, success, happiness, resiliency, and self-directedness

Graduates shared that throughout this reengagement process, meaningful connections between them and adults at MMC were central to the speed and level of successful turnaround. Educator behaviors characterized by forgiveness, patience, love, high expectations, respect, and humor were cited by many graduates as key contributors to their metamorphosis. More than any other element for success, the former MMC students attributed their turnaround to the MMC teachers' caring attitudes, faithful friendships, and concrete acts of kindness toward them. All graduates' most often stated the reason for this change was the "caring actions and atmosphere" perceived by the students as present at MMC.

In closing

I have gained a few personal insights from my inside-out view as MMC's founding principal and from my outside-in view as a postgraduate student. I have adopted guidelines for myself that I recommend to others:

1. Take the time to investigate best practices and sound theoretical principles, and work to blend the selected insights with your own practical field experience.
2. Trust all teachers with the responsibility to create, deliver, and assess curriculum.
3. Understand that because something is perceived as having a cause-effect relationship does not necessarily mean that it does.
4. Investigate all elements of the school (that is, teachers, students, parents, administrators, secretaries, and others), as well as the interactions that take place between and among these parts of the whole.
5. Trust that the learners themselves are our richest resource as we explore the fragile and complex process of student engagement, disengagement, and reengagement.
6. Insist upon providing counseling training to all school staff and develop your school around a carefully selected guidance base.
7. Accept that educators do have the ability to purposefully establish and protect certain school-related factors that positively influence student engagement or reengagement.

References

Barth, R. *Improving Schools from Within*. San Francisco: Jossey-Bass, 1990.
Curwin, R., and Mendler, A. *Discipline with Dignity*. Alexandria, Va.: ASCD, 1988.
Glasser, W. *Control Theory in the Classroom*. New York: HarperCollins, 1986.
Guskey, T. *Implementing Mastery Learning*. Belmont, Calif.: Wadsworth, 1985.
Lieberman, J. "High Risk Students Make Big Gains." *Journal of Cooperative Education*, 1986, 58–65.
Marzano, R., and others. *Dimensions of Learning*. Alexandria, Va.: ASCD, 1992.
Purkey, W., and Nowak, J. *Inviting School Success*. Belmont, Calif.: Wadsworth, 1984.
Sergiovanni, T. *Moral Leadership: Getting to the Heart of School Improvement*. San Francisco: Jossey-Bass, 1992.

CHERY S. WAGONLANDER, *principal of Mott Middle College and adjunct instructor at Ferris State and Eastern Michigan Universities, specializes in K–12 school reform. She consults with schools in the areas of collaboration, curriculum development, and drop-out prevention.*

Research has found a positive relationship between teachers'
sense of efficacy and students' classroom achievement. When
teachers believe they can influence student learning, they usu-
ally do. Reluctant learners, students who are unwilling to put
forth effort and take risk to improve academically, need teach-
ers who believe in their capacity to find the right strategy to
motivate their students to learn.

8

Reluctant learners need high-efficacy teachers

Diane Jackson

ROBERT JONES, A THIRTEEN-YEAR-OLD eighth-grader at True Middle School, has earned the reputation of class clown. He tells jokes throughout the school day and seizes every opportunity to imitate or mock others. This behavior tends to be contrary to the way his friends perceive him in his neighborhood. He is an attractive, aggressive, articulate, intense, unmotivated, low performer.

A shadow of Robert's day in school reveals many interesting characteristics and behaviors. Often and without explanation, he arrives to school late. He enters his first hour loud and disruptive. Once there, he refuses to do the work. After repeated coaching by many of his teachers, he gives up his attitude and completes minimal tasks. On rare occasions, he will give his teachers a glimpse of what he can do academically. He often states that the work is too hard, and he just can't get it. He gives up easily when faced with a challenge and reacts bitterly when he receives a poor grade. He is

NEW DIRECTIONS FOR SCHOOL LEADERSHIP, NO. 6, WINTER 1997 © JOSSEY-BASS PUBLISHERS

quick to acknowledge that he knew he would fail. Many teachers have heard him say that the work they ask him to do is dumb. He refuses to look at his test scores as information that can help him do better, and he puts forth very little effort to improve.

Robert entered the eighth grade with a paper trail from his sixth- and seventh-grade classes. Most of the data reflects his current state: lacks motivation, undisciplined, doesn't care about learning. Robert's sixth-grade records revealed some interesting data. His academic performance started out good to fair but progressively declined during the school year. Further investigation by the school administrator found that Robert was a good to excellent student in elementary school. It was obvious that nothing was wrong with Robert academically. Shortly before entering middle school, Robert revealed his fear of failure. He believed middle school would prove too difficult for him and had every expectation of failure. Conferences held with Robert's parents confirmed the fears he expressed. They had noticed the decline in his grades and behavior but were at a loss as to what to do. They had tried many strategies with him, to no avail.

Robert's homeroom class is known as the "troublemakers." Many teachers in his school do not enjoy working with this group. In fact, many of them feel the students don't have the skills to do the work. Busy work has become the course of the day. Students are presented with materials below their grade level and rewarded for the outcomes. Many students know this but don't complain. When some of the teachers who believe that they can perform well gave them challenging work, the students claimed it was too difficult. Robert's voice was heard loud and clear. Many of Robert's teachers have given up on him. He has become a reluctant learner, a student unwilling to put forth effort and take risk to improve academically.

Robert enjoys the reputation that his homeroom class has earned. It has given him a sense of power. He told a friend, "We may not be all that [smart], but we know how to control this school."

Could Robert's profile fit 20 to 30 percent of young adolescent males in middle schools? How can we help Robert and others like him to be successful in school?

This chapter takes a look at students like Robert who give up on themselves academically, and at what teachers can to do to enable them to perform at higher capacity. For many years as an elementary and middle school teacher in Detroit Public Schools, I learned how to motivate children and keep them excited about learning. Later, I became a staff developer and had the responsibility to support new teachers, especially experienced teachers who were not trained to address the inner-city child.

Characteristics of reluctant learners

Many young students enter preschool and kindergarten with a thirst for learning. They tackle complex tasks and don't seem afraid of failure. Observe these same children a few years later as they sit in elementary and middle-school classrooms, however, and one sees a different picture. For many, motivation is now a problem. Attention strays, minds wander. Extrinsic incentives and sanctions are now required to motivate children to learn their assigned lessons. Many begin to behave like Robert.

What has happened to these formerly excited, curious, intrinsically motivated children? They have been impacted upon and enveloped by a system that necessarily constrains and standardizes their learning opportunities. Little or no creativity is required. Much of school revolves around a hidden curriculum of social control and classroom management. Children spend many hours in crowded classrooms waiting, in transition from one classroom to another, and in passive observation of the teacher's interactions with other students (Dreeben, 1968; Winnett and Winkler, 1972).

As a result, motivation has become a problem for many students in our educational system. It was for Robert. Indeed, though it is a difficult claim to evaluate, there is some evidence to suggest that such effects may be cumulative through the years. Harter (1981), for example, has found that as students move from third through ninth grade they prefer activities that are less intrinsically motivated and more extrinsically motivated. The older the students the more likely they are to indicate, for instance, that they would prefer a simple but boring task that makes it easier to accomplish minimal standards. These minimal successes are encouraged with high extrinsic rewards. The misuse of overly powerful extrinsic rewards and sanctions may unwittingly undermine children's intrinsic motivation (Lepper and Hodell, 1989), but it is a common practice in elementary schools where students are showered with stickers and stars. By the time students reach middle school they find fewer such extrinsic rewards, so they begin to question their intellectual capability.

Middle school requires more effort and less extrinsic reinforcement. At this stage, many students begin to wonder if they have what it takes to be successful. Could this be Robert's problem? Did elementary school overly reward him with extrinsic rewards and hamper his ability to accurately assess his capabilities? Was his academic success in elementary school a result of hard work or of easy work and powerful extrinsic rewards? Has middle school presented him with challenges where intrinsic motivation is needed for him to sustain his effort? Does he have the motivation to improve? Let's continue to analyze the scenario to find out.

Fixed intelligence versus effort

There is evidence that middle school teachers use a stricter standard than elementary school teachers to assess student competency and to evaluate student performance. This could pose a problem for students whose level of effort toward a task has not changed. If teachers apply stricter standards, but students put forth the same or a lesser amount of effort as before, failure will become the only reality for many of them. How will students explain this failure to themselves? What impact will this have on them? Will they begin to question their capacity to learn?

Implicit theories of intelligence are beliefs about the fundamental nature of intelligence. Specifically, people tend to think that intelligence is fixed and cannot be changed (an entity or innate ability theory) or that it is malleable and can be increased through effort (an incremental or process theory). Both are powerful assumptions about the distribution of intelligence and its relationship to learning capacity. The major premise is that intelligence is unequally distributed within what is considered the normal population, that some individuals are highly intelligent ("vs"—very smart), some moderately so ("ss"—sorta smart), and some not very bright at all ("kd"—kinda dumb). These beliefs constitute a paradigm—a more or less universally accepted and taken-for-granted theory that organizes perception and behavior. At its core is the belief that intelligence controls the capacity of an individual to develop intellectually. Intelligence is thought to be an innate endowment, fixed at birth and apportioned to different people in different quantities (Howard, 1991).

The question is whether these beliefs about intelligence affect students' performance in school. Dweck (1990) has found a difference between the ways incremental and entity theorists approach academic tasks. A recent study indicates a link between these beliefs and grades develops when students move into middle school. Henderson, Dweck, and Chiu (1992) questioned 229 entering seventh graders about intelligence. Nearly two-thirds (139) showed a consistent preference for either an entity or an incremental theory. The researchers then used another measure to divide the students in each group into those with high and low confidence in their own abilities.

Comparing students' grades and achievement test scores in sixth grade with their seventh-grade report cards, Henderson and Dweck (1995) found some surprises. They expected that entity theorists who had been low achievers would remain so. But many of those who had performed well in sixth grade and had entered the seventh grade confident of their abilities were now receiving grades below those predicted by previous performance. Meanwhile, incrementalists maintained their performance at a level equal to or better than their elementary school grades. Even those who had not done especially well in sixth grade—and had begun seventh grade with low confidence—matched or exceeded their predicted performance. Perhaps most surprising, the low-confidence incrementalists earned higher grades than the high-confidence entity theorists.

In fact, students who held entity theories and had high confidence at the start of seventh grade showed the most pronounced decline of any group. When Henderson did a follow-up study of these same kids at the end of eighth grade, she found continued low performance. They had not recovered from the seventh-grade slump.

To explain this decline, Dweck looks at the way children answer the question, "When do you feel smart?" Incrementalists cite times when they put effort into something, when they don't understand something and then get it, or when they figure out something new. In contrast, entity theorists point to times when a task is easy for them, when not much effort is required, when they do not make mistakes, or when they finish first (Dweck, 1990).

Insofar as learning involves putting effort into challenging tasks, entity theorists are caught in a serious bind. What they do to feel smart and what they must do to learn new things are at odds. For the past decade, Dweck and her colleagues have investigated why and how some children end up in this bind. Dweck has identified two distinct, coherent patterns in ways children approach difficult academic tasks.

Mastery versus performance goals

In the maladaptive or "helpless" pattern, children define themselves as having failed soon after reaching a difficult problem, usually attributing their difficulties to a lack of ability and predicting poor future performance. Children manifesting a more mastery-oriented, adaptive pattern respond to difficulty by issuing more self-instructions and by planning strategies to overcome failures. In the same experiment, many of these students spontaneously expressed confidence that they would succeed in the future. Twenty-five percent began to use more sophisticated problem-solving strategies than evidenced in earlier, simpler tasks; in all, 80 percent of the mastery-oriented children maintained or improved their strategies as the tasks got more difficult (Hong, Chiu, and Dweck, 1995).

These researchers discovered that the two groups focus on different goals, which can lead them to construe and react to events differently. Those who believe that intelligence is a fixed trait tend to pursue the aim of proving they have it. Setting what Dweck calls performance goals, entity theorists seek positive evaluations of their abilities and try to avoid negative ones.

In one experiment, children who focused on performance goals rejected the chance to learn something new if it involved any risk of error or confusion. They seemed vulnerable to losing confidence in themselves and thus falling into the helplessness pattern. In contrast, children who focus on mastery and set learning goals are likely to persist in the face of difficulty. They see effort as something that activates ability rather than as an indicator of low ability. When facing challenging academic tasks, they view these as opportunities to get smarter—a much more adaptive response (Hong, Chiu, and Dweck, 1995).

So could it be that Robert believed in an entity theory, that his ability was fixed at birth, and each failure validated for him his lack of intelligence? After he experienced a failure, did he explain it to himself in a way that debilitated his effort? Did he spend most of his time trying to prove his adequacy instead of improving so learning could occur?

Students like Robert show us that we need a new approach to education; one that will give our children the solid base of knowledge, skills, and confidence they will need to meet the challenges of their time. An alternative paradigm, a new framework about development based on the simple proposition that all children can learn—once they are taught how—will help teachers reorganize their thinking and their practices. A new framework will start with an empowering idea of what intelligence or development is: a process of building capability (Howard, 1991). We must begin to look at how the organization and structure of the classroom shapes and socializes adaptive and maladaptive motivation patterns. Teachers must investigate the possible negative effects of such daily evaluative practices with children, including extrinsic rewards, ability grouping, and a focus on how quickly they respond (Ames and Ames, 1990).

As a first step, we can examine the role of teacher expectations in student learning. Research shows that teachers must believe that they can influence how well students learn—especially difficult students or those who are not motivated—and students must believe that they have the capacity to learn at very high levels. Teachers who believe that they can make a difference in their student's performance have a high sense of self-efficacy (Weber and Omotani, 1994).

Numerous studies have found a positive relationship between the teacher's sense of efficacy and the students' classroom achievement. In fact, researchers call teacher efficacy the single most powerful "explanatory variable" in student performance. It's not surprising, then, that high-efficacy teachers typically produce high-achieving students, and low-efficacy teachers tend to produce lower-achieving students (Weber and Omotani, 1994). The real question is why.

One reason appears to be that teachers with a low sense of efficacy place responsibility for learning on the students. When students fail, these teachers look for explanations in nonschool factors, such as ability, motivation, or family background. Teachers with a high sense of efficacy, in contrast, take personal responsibility for students' learning. When students fail, these teachers examine their own performance and look for ways they might have been more helpful. The more responsible a teacher feels for making sure students learn, the less likely that the teacher will give up in the face of students' difficulty—and, more important, less likely to convey to the child that he or she is inadequate or incapable.

Low-efficacy teachers versus high-efficacy teachers

Characteristics of low-efficacy teachers take their toll on student achievement. In a report prepared for the U.S. Department of Education's National Institute of Education, researchers P. T. Ashton, R. B. Webb, and N. Doda (1982) arrived at the following findings:

- Low-efficacy teachers hold low academic standards for low-achieving students; in contrast, high-efficacy teachers hold higher standards for the same students.
- Low-efficacy teachers are less likely to monitor the on-task behavior of low-achieving students, whereas high-efficacy teachers concentrate on academics and insist that all students remain on task.
- Low-efficacy teachers tend to have negative attitudes toward low-achieving students (seeing them, for example, as threatening) and tend to use negative means of controlling them. High-efficacy teachers are more likely to define low-achieving students as reachable, teachable, and worthy of attention and are more likely to build friendly, unthreatening relationships with them.
- Low-efficacy teachers tend to sort and stratify their classes according to ability and concentrate their efforts and affection on high-achieving students.

In the classrooms of low-efficacy teachers, then, it's logical that already successful students continue to achieve, while students who are having difficulty continue to struggle or fail—the result of minimal effort and low expectations on the part of the teacher. It's a self-fulfilling prophecy: good students get better, and poor students get worse (Weber and Omotami, 1994).

When low-efficacy teachers perceive that students have different abilities, their treatment of each student is dissimilar as well; this then leads to variances in student's behavior and ultimately variances in their achievement. Not surprisingly, high efficacy on the teacher's part usually goes hand in hand with high achievement on the part of students.

Helping Robert succeed

It appears that Robert Jones, like many adolescents, may have learned how to give up on himself. He became a reluctant learner, a student unwilling to put forth effort and risk to improve. He may have experienced a difficult transition from elementary to middle school; higher standards and a withdrawal of extrinsic rewards made him begin to doubt his intellectual development. He may have begun to experience failure and attributed the failure inappropriately, to a lack of ability. Repeated failure validated for him his "kinda dumb" fixed status.

Low teacher expectation, ineffective instruction, and no motivation to improve may have placed Robert in a situation where he is reluctant to learn. What does Robert need? He needs a teacher who has a high sense of efficacy. Students need teachers who believe in them and teachers who believe in their own capacity to teach. They need teachers who understand student transitions, theories of intelligence, instructional strategies, classroom management techniques, and the needs of young men like Robert. They need teachers who can motivate, stimulate, engage, discipline, and empower students. They need teachers who have a high sense of efficacy, who do the following:

1. Set high standards for self and students
2. Take personal responsibility for students' learning
3. When students fail, examine their own performance for improvement
4. Concentrate on academics and insist that all students remain on task.

How does a teacher attain a high sense of efficacy? My current role as an educational consultant gives me an opportunity to help teachers develop a high sense of efficacy. Staff development is structured to help teachers recognize the difference between teaching efficacy (which results from believing that all students can learn) and personal efficacy (which results when a teacher has confidence in his or her ability to teach students effectively). Staff development seeks to cultivate high teaching efficacy, offering appropriate corrective strategies for teachers who doubt their students' ability to learn, and high personal efficacy, offering corrective strategies for teachers who question their own abilities. This difference becomes very important as we look at teachers' attitudes, behaviors, beliefs, and their impact on student achievement.

Personal efficacy

If the sense of personal efficacy is high, students will perform well because the teacher believes that it's possible; but if a teacher's sense of personal efficacy is low, it becomes very difficult to teach students and help them to perform well in school. One phase of the staff development effort to create a high sense of efficacy is to take a close look at beliefs and their impact on one's effort. The Efficacy Institute, Inc., where I consult, helps teachers explore their current belief about intelligence and its impact on effort (theirs and students'). Teachers are guided through a process of awareness, reflection, and action to make changes. They are challenged to consider that all students are capable of learning at the highest levels, and tools are provided to help them help students change the way they think about intelligence and failure. The corrective strategies include the following:

- *Exploring beliefs about intelligence.* All students can learn, all teachers can teach.
- *Finding one's locus of control.* Teachers have control over the instructional and behavioral strategies they use; if they aren't working, change them.
- *Perceiving failure as feedback.* Failure provides information that can lead to improvement. The teacher should wonder, What must I do differently next time?
- *Developing short- and long-term goals to monitor improvement.*

Teachers are guided through a variety of classroom experiences to help them to see their capability and enhance their sense of efficacy.

Instructional-teacher efficacy

The second phase of the staff development component is to take a close look at teachers' relationship with students, classroom management strategies, their instructional strategies, and their impact on high teacher efficacy. Teachers are taught how to build relationships with students, how to get to know them and communicate to them that school is a place where success can occur. Teachers are given strategies to demonstrate to students that they care, to have friendly conversations with them, and to build warm relationships with them. Here is an example of actual classroom practices that can move a reluctant learner like Robert to success:

Goal setting for a classroom

It's Monday morning inside Mrs. Robinson's Language Arts eighth grade classroom. The class period begins with thirty-five students divided into small groups, discussing their academic and behavioral goals for the week. Challenges and obstacles that could stop them from being successful are explored so that they will have a successful week. Action steps are laid out:

1. *Start.* What do you want to aim for?
2. *Plan.* How will you do it?
3. *Measure.* Where are you now?
4. *Write.* Write a short statement saying exactly what you want to achieve.
5. *Time.* Set a time or date for completion.
6. *Do.* Stop and picture yourself making your goal.
7. *Evaluate.* Did you hit the mark?

Then each group comes to a consensus on the final steps.

Mrs. Robinson brings the groups together for a large group discussion. The goal-setting process and the support that it provides for the students are discussed. She reinforces the expectation that the classroom is a community of learners, everyone coming together to support the academic success for the individual. This is a weekly practice in Mrs. Robinson's classroom. All of her students get an opportunity to review their goals with other students. They are encouraged to recognize and discuss their individual and group outcomes. The goal is success for all. Why? Because Mrs. Robinson is a high-efficacy teacher.

Conclusion

Careful, intentional relationship building becomes the foundation for easier classroom management. Teachers who have a high sense of efficacy are not afraid to build relationships with students and understand how powerful it can be for guiding behavior. Good classroom management strategies include developing clear and fair classroom expectations instead of rules, enforcing consequences consistently and without anger, structuring classroom meetings, and using peer coaching and mediation.

Disciplined students are ready to learn, so instructional strategies must be conducive to learning. Some of these strategies are to write objectives at the application level; to activate prior knowledge and construct meaning; to model, demonstrate, or show when teaching something new; to teach incrementally by breaking all objectives down into small steps; and to use a variety of assessment tools. The research literature on teacher efficacy shows that teachers who believe they can make a difference do make a difference. Reluctant learners need high-efficacy teachers—teachers who will not give up on them and will help them to find out how good they can become.

Teachers must become coaches for students. Excellent coaches have a high sense of efficacy. Like that of a good athletic coach, the job of the educator-coach is not to decide whether the student-team has the basic ability required to play the game but to assume that each student can meet the challenges of an aggressive curriculum; the measure of the educator is his or her success in coaching each student to use the process of development (teaching incrementally) to meet the challenge (Efficacy Institute, 1993).

We can encourage reluctant learners to become successful learners if we become very intentional, systematic, and procedural about what we do as teachers and engineer success for all of our students. The Robert Joneses in our schools deserve it, and teachers with a high sense of efficacy understand it.

References

Ames, R., and Ames, C. "Adolescent Motivation and Achievement." In J. Worell and F. Danner (eds.), *Adolescent Development: Issues for Education.* New York: Academic Press, 1990.

Ashton, P. T., Webb, R. B., and Doda, N. *A Study of Teachers' Sense of Efficacy: Final Report.* (Vol. 1). Washington, D.C.: National Institute of Education, U.S. Department of Education, 1982.

Dreeben, R. *On What Is Learned in School.* Reading, Mass.: Addison-Wesley, 1968.

Dweck, C. S. "Self Theories and Goals: Their Role in Motivation, Personality, and Development." Unpublished paper, Columbia University, 1990.

Efficacy Institute. Trainer's manual. Lexington, Mass.: Efficacy Institute, 1993.

Harter, S. "A New Self-Report Scale of Intrinsic Versus Extrinsic Orientation in the Classroom: Motivational and Developmental Component." *Developmental Psychology,* 1981, *17*, 300–312.

Henderson, V., and Dweck, C. S. "Adolescence and Achievement." In S. Feldman and G. Elliott (eds.), *At the Threshold: Adolescent Development.* Cambridge, Mass.: Harvard University Press, 1995.

Henderson, V., Dweck, C. S., and Chiu, C. A Measure of Implicit Theories of Intelligence. Unpublished manuscript. New York: Columbia University, 1992.

Hong, Y., Chiu, C., and Dweck, C. "Implicit Theories of Intelligence: Reconsidering the Role of Confidence in Achievement Motivation." In M. Kernis (ed.), *Efficacy, Agency, and Self-Esteem.* New York: Plenum, 1995.

Howard, J. "Getting Smart: The Social Construction of Intelligence." Paper submitted to the Efficacy Institute, Inc., Lexington, Mass., 1991.

Lepper, R. M., and Hodell, M. "Intrinsic Motivation in the Classroom." *Research on Motivation in Education,* 1989, *3,* 73–101.

Weber, B. J., and Omotani, L. M. "The Power of Believing." *Executive Educator,* 1994, *16* (9), 35–38.

Winnett, R., and Winkler, R. "Current Behavior Modification in the Classroom: Be Still, Be Quiet, Be Docile." *Journal of Applied Behavior Analysis,* 1972, *5,* 499–504.

DIANE JACKSON, *a former teacher and staff developer for many years in the Detroit Public Schools, is currently the senior schools service coordinator with the Efficacy Institute in Lexington, Massachusetts.*

The phenomenon of throw-away children is viewed as stemming from self-disconnection. A new model of change in education is proposed that begins by first reconnecting adults to their own core self.

9

The power of self-connection: transforming adults to reclaim the children

Pamela Gerloff

WHERE I GREW UP in northern Illinois, farm kids weren't supposed to do well in school. (The stereotype of the "dumb farmer" was alive and well.) Being from a farm I always knew this, but I had a stubborn streak, so I figured I would show those teachers that what they believed wasn't true. Besides, I went to a school system that was as good as any I've seen, and I found plenty there to engage me: writing, art, music, science projects, ethical dilemmas, the drama of injustice, active games, and occasional time outdoors by the trees and the creek. Something I always knew, though, just beneath the surface of my awareness, was that life at school was never as vital, as real, or as genuine as life at home with my family. And at school, I could never really relax. There were always too many people, and people whom I didn't really know. And somebody was always watching us, assessing us.

By standard definitions, I was not a throw-away kid. I did well in school, even thrived there. I got top grades, was involved in

NEW DIRECTIONS FOR SCHOOL LEADERSHIP, NO. 6, WINTER 1997 © JOSSEY-BASS PUBLISHERS

extracurricular activities, held leadership positions. Most importantly, I was able to find meaning in much of what I did. I was able to find a way to connect to school that kept both my intellect and spirit alive. And yet even in me something was lost, thrown away, in all those countless, agonizing hours when I was made to stay attentive to what did not draw me.

Others did not fare so well. Some kids, bright as they were, simply could not stomach school—and regularly let it be known. Some merely endured, awaiting their release at the end of each day. And some tried very hard to fit in but for one reason or another just couldn't make it in the system. Among the saddest of these was Eduardo (not his real name), a Hispanic boy who rode my bus to school. The son of migrant workers, he would come north every year with his family during the harvesting season, returning to Texas during the winter. Everybody liked Eduardo; he was personable, happy, and engaging. I remember that he was always so quick-minded, so eager to learn and explore and engage the world. One day, however, shortly after the harvest season had begun, I was sitting on the school bus wondering why Eduardo wasn't riding it this year. We had just pulled up to the elementary school to let the little kids off before we went on to the high school when I noticed a familiar face staring blankly out the window of another bus. It was Eduardo, his eyes vacant and expressionless, riding the special education bus. I found out later that this native Spanish speaker had been given a standardized test in English and then shunted away from the friends and teachers and activities he loved.

Then, of course, there was the popular, economically well-off classmate of my brother's, who committed suicide shortly after high school.

As I contemplate these and other school experiences, I ask myself these questions: Who among these are the throw-away children? What in them got thrown away? And who, or what, is responsible?

The answers are not entirely obvious, because in the public schools I went to it wasn't as if we had poor teachers, apathetic parents, a substandard curriculum, inadequate facilities and resources, or leaders devoid of vision or leadership. On the contrary, we had caring teachers who put in extra hours for their students (even if they did fall victim to common stereotypes); principals who knew all the kids in the school; an elementary school superintendent so sought after that he was soon hired away to a big-city school district out east; team teaching; innovative scheduling; a rich curriculum; books; a beautiful, well-designed building and grounds; and parents who spent time with their children.

Redefining "throw-away kids"

As my interest in education developed, I taught and observed in other school systems and I began to notice two things:

1. In *every* school, without fail, there was always a certain number of kids who seemed to get next to nothing out of school, kids for whom school was either meaningless or essentially worthless.
2. No matter how good the school system or how few throwaways it appeared to have, *something was missing*—even in those kids who seemed to do well in the system. Something seemed to be lost, weakened, or destroyed in them.

Over time, I have come to understand that what was lost or thrown away in all these children was *connection*—a connection to *themselves*, to their own spirit, life energy, aliveness, confidence, joy, and especially to a *knowing or sense of their own life purpose*.

I had had intimations of this when I was still quite young. One day in my fourth-grade classroom, I was standing at the side of the room checking my math paper against the answer sheet we consulted when we had completed our work. As I was doing this, an awareness came over me. It came as a knowing, a knowing that I had a purpose in life. But along with this came perplexity, for I was also aware that though I knew I had a particular purpose, I didn't know what it was. So I went back to grading my math.

This incident is telling to me, because as I contemplate it I recall that even at that young age I knew there was something larger and grander to life, but my life in school was somehow disconnected from it.

I now know that other children have these kinds of experiences, too, though as adults they may not readily remember them. At various points in their school life, children become aware that what goes on at school is disconnected from why they are really here, in life. And at these points of awareness they make an internal decision about how they will respond to the situation. Most of the time, the decision involves disconnecting from one's own aliveness, awareness, and deepest passions—or at least hiding them so others won't see.

My own belief is that self-disconnection happens to all children in school, whether they are recognized as throw-away children or not—*because it is designed right into the system*. Gatto (1992) delineated some of the ways that schools, by virtue of the way they are organized and operated, rob children of intimate connection to themselves. Students have little or no private time, are under almost constant surveillance from an adult, are continually evaluated and judged, and have few if any intimate relationships with others in school.

In my view, the difference between students who are recognized by educators as throw-away children and those who are not is simply this: recognized throw-aways have disconnected not only from themselves but also from the school system. They have either disconnected on their own, or the system itself has cut them off. Unrecognized throw-aways have disconnected as well—not from the system but from themselves.

Thus, my definition of throw-away children is *children who have lost connection to themselves*. Because the very nature and structure of schools as we currently know them creates self-disconnection, every kid in our schools is a throw-away kid to one degree or another. The deepest, most valuable part of a child is simply thrown away in school.

If this is so, what do we do?

Realigning our intention

To eliminate throw-away kids—both recognized and unrecognized—altogether, I believe we need to begin from a different premise than heretofore we have had in designing our schools. We need to create schools with a different underlying purpose or intention in mind.

What if we created schools to support the unfoldment of each person's unique life purpose?

What if we created schools to support each child's connection to a deeper self?

What if schools existed to help children discover and accomplish their fondest dreams?

What if the purpose of schools were to help children develop their unique gifts and talents and use them to serve humanity?

Chopra (1993) has written about "the law of 'dharma' or purpose in life" (p. 93). Variations of this principle have been recognized throughout history by a variety of philosophies, religions, and codes of living. In Chopra's words, "Everyone has a purpose in life . . . a unique gift or special talent to give to others. And when we blend this unique talent with service to others, we experience the ecstasy and exultation of our own spirit, which is the ultimate goal of all goals" (p. 93).

Schools as a reflection of our own fears

If schools were genuinely designed around this principle, then throw-away kids—both as I define them and as schools define them now—would no longer exist. As it is, schools were never designed to serve the purpose Chopra describes. In fact, my observations suggest that schools were (unconsciously) designed to work against that very principle. Why? Because as a collective we have not been ready to handle the energy and power that would be released if large numbers of our children were allowed to connect fully to themselves, and from that connection to develop and express themselves with their full capacities, power, and creativity, fully aligned with their own unique purpose in life.

Think about it. Although we often claim as a society that we want our children to develop their full potential, what would we do if they did? What would we do with the creative ideas that would emerge to challenge our current thinking? With the solutions they would come up with to problems we don't really want to go away? With the excitement in living that would stand as a continual reminder to the rest of us that our own lives don't resound at any-where near those decibels of joy? Psychologist Abraham Maslow (1971) wrote of what he called "the Jonah complex"—humans' innate fear of becoming their best self. *What if schools as we know them are a manifestation of our collective fear of becoming our best self?* If that were true, schools would need to be inherently designed to keep us from connecting to that self of which we are so afraid. And throw-away kids would be a natural and inevitable result of that design.

Throughout history, society has always found ways to crush the vital energy expressed so naturally in children. As a collective, we've come up with some pretty effective ways to keep the lid on. The harsh conditions of child labor during the industrial era are just one example. But modern-day schooling, which is explicitly modeled after the factory conditions of the industrial revolution (Callahan, 1962; Conrad, 1951), is one of the cleverest means we as a collec-tive have yet devised—because it *looks* so innocuous, even noble. Sweatshops didn't last too long, relatively speaking, because they were obviously brutal. But modern-day schools, with their noble-sounding mission statements, their broad range of curricular and extracurricular offerings, their professional development trainings, innovative alternative programs, computer labs, well-groomed lawns and football fields, lull us into believing our own rhetoric. We literally cannot see that our "factory model" of schooling—with its large classes, compartmentalized instruction, bells delineating arbitrarily set work periods, and its still-predominant metaphor of pouring instruction into waiting containers where everyone must be treated the same to come out equal—serves the same purpose of confining the bursting spirit of our children as child labor did a century ago. The modern-day factory of school may be less brutal to the body but perhaps not less brutal to the spirit.

Creating change

Many people in a variety of fields have observed that we are no longer an industrial society. "Postmodern era," "postindustrial society," and "information age" are all labels now routinely used to describe the times we live in. Some have suggested that with this shift in our culture has come a new necessity for and a new openness to people developing their unique abilities, gifts, and talents and sharing them with the collective. But such a shift cannot occur within the present educational structure—unless the structure changes to support a new purpose.

How do we do that?

One way is to actually begin to create schools that start from a new underlying premise. Attempts to shift the fundamental purpose and structure of schools are not new. Alternative forms of education have emerged over and over again throughout the history of modern schooling. However, they rarely extend beyond an individual school or endure for very long. Nor do they go beyond the bounds of what is acceptable to the larger system. (Even the current charter school movement imposes on schools restrictions that prevent approval of models of education that fall too far outside the established norm.) Our system of modern education has proved highly resistant to significant alteration of its basic structure and purpose. Put simply, we have not been able to step out of our old paradigms in our collective thinking about education.

If we really want to eliminate throw-away children altogether, we need to find a way to shift the purpose of our school system on a larger scale than is commonly attempted so that small-scale changes that do occur can continue to thrive within the larger system. In essence, we need to create a new paradigm. To do that, we need to find a means of reform that is so gentle and organic that it bypasses the resistance mechanisms inherent in the system as it currently exists.

A tall order—but what if it's possible?

Although it is essential that we begin to reformulate our concepts of schooling—and out of that reformation create entirely new structures—I believe that no significant, lasting change is possible in schools unless the adults who are involved in them begin to live and act from a fundamentally new way of being. Only a shift of mind can bring about a shift of form. Consequently, my view is that a necessary first step is to begin our movements toward transformation not with schools but with the adults who work in them. To that end, I am developing a program (called the *Querencia* program) designed specifically for adults who work in or for schools—teachers, administrators, staff members, volunteers, school board members, and others who feel called to participate.

Querencia: The experience of self-connection

The purpose of the program is to reconnect the adults in schools to their own core self—to their own life purpose, their deep joy, their intuitive knowing: to the inner impulse of their heart. I call this place of connection *querencia* (pronounced *kay-REN-see-ah*). *Querencia* is a Spanish word used in bullfighting to refer to the one spot in the bull ring where the bull feels completely safe and completely powerful. That place of safe haven is different for each bull and for each fight. Every bullfighter fears it, for if the bull finds that spot he becomes fearless and unbeatable (Remen, 1996).

Similarly, in each of us there is a space or state of awareness where we feel completely safe, completely powerful, completely protected, and completely content. It is from this space of awareness that our unique life purpose, our destiny, our deepest longing, and our greatest joy arise. This is our *querencia*.

People from widely differing traditions and disciplines have referred to this inner connection or state of awareness using a variety of terms (such as center, inner self, core self, inner voice, intuitive knowing, flow). Although these different words may not always refer to precisely the same phenomenon, it is clear that the connection to one's own deeper awareness has been recognized throughout history. Individually, we have all had profound moments of such connection, perhaps experienced as a deep sense of peace or joy or intense aliveness; times when we have felt profoundly connected, content, and whole. When we are in that state, our sense of time may be altered—it may seem not to exist at all, or it flies by unnoticed or slows practically to a halt. We may experience our actions and their results as effortless, as if something else is doing them through us or as if some unseen hand is assisting their unfoldment. Or we may simply experience a profound absorption in the moment at hand.

As children, we experience this state quite naturally, and often. My own memories of such times include summer evenings gazing at beautiful sunsets, quiet moments alone petting a kitten, doing chores on our family farm, practicing a challenging piano piece, building tunnels in the hay mow with my siblings. For me, the experience of *querencia* comes most often as a feeling of deep inner silence, what I call the quiet of the heart.

Losing the connection

Every child knows intimately the experience of self-connection. However, as we grow older and begin to acclimate to our surrounding culture we encounter impediments to this connection, resulting in an increasing sense of struggle, discontent, and fragmentation. In my case, the most pronounced impediments occurred in school. (These were also the most insidious, because they were prolonged and subtle to detect.) Some simple yet potent examples are the repeated interruptions to classroom activities that regularly occurred in school, preventing deep absorption in the moment; constant external judgment and evaluation, which diverted attention from internal awareness, requiring instead a constant vigilance of attention to external sources of approval; and an inability to pursue activities with which I was deeply captivated because of the need to follow a prescribed curriculum according to a preset timetable.

The profound significance of such disrupted self-connection has been noted by Csikszentmihalyi, a psychologist and researcher who has extensively studied the phenomenon of "flow" or "optimal human experience." He reports that the key to attaining and maintaining flow lies in the ability to control attention, or psychic energy. He notes, "When a person cannot control psychic energy, neither learning nor true enjoyment is possible" (1990, p. 84). (This, he explains, is the difficulty faced by schoolchildren identified as having attention disorders.) He also observes that this experience of flow gives our lives a sense of meaning and purpose. In other words, the ability to experience flow—which derives from what I call self-connection, or *querencia*—is the essential ingredient not only in learning but in the ability to experience happiness and meaning in life.

The experience of effortless flow

In addition to the essential role that self-connection plays in learning and in the ability to find happiness and meaning in life I have observed that it is from the connection to the *querencia* that lasting change occurs, both individually and collectively. When individuals become more deeply connected to their own life purpose, their life begins to unfold anew, according to its own unique design. As Keith Varnum (personal communication with the author, July 1997) has noted, it is as if the *querencia* (which he calls our "knowing") contains a blueprint for our own life's destiny. Consequently, when we connect deeply to our *querencia*, then our life purpose (which is also our greatest joy) reveals itself and begins to unfold naturally, "with no effort or doingness." Jaworski (1996) describes this same phenomenon and explains it from a scientific perspective.

In my teaching of writing, I have noticed this quality of effortless unfoldment when students connect more deeply to themselves while writing. This is true both for students in regular school settings and for individual clients. Creating an environment that allows absorption in the writing process, coupled with tools that enable students to free their attention and connect to their own self, produces remarkable results—both in the quality of students' writing and in their ease and enjoyment of the writing process.

The experience of effortless transformation can also occur in a whole-school setting as a result of individual practitioners' connection to their *querencia*. This is evident in the case of Linda, a charter school administrator who participated in workshops designed to facilitate self-connection. Linda was responsible for leading teacher meetings in her school. Although she made no particular effort at these meetings to bring about school change, she did speak and act from her own *querencia*, and she consciously treated others in the school with a genuine sense of equality, as she had experienced in the workshops. Viewing each teacher as equal to herself and to the other teachers, she recognized that each of their contributions were of equal value to the school. Says Linda, "We were equals coming together at a round table. I honored the natural energies of each person in the room."

Each teacher thus had significant input into what became a process of creating a vision for the new charter school. Together, the group was able to reach a consensus about a vision for their school—and, once their collective beliefs and visions were aligned as a group, the school developed in that direction. As Linda experienced it, this process occurred naturally and with ease, a seeming effortlessness. The school simply changed because, she said, "How teachers managed their classrooms changed, and this caused students to change."

Nurturing connection in self and other

This example also illustrates a phenomenon that, though subtle, promises to be a powerful mechanism for school change: when adults are strongly connected to their own *querencia*, they are able to value and nurture that connection in their colleagues and students, as well as themselves. Their own self-connection gives rise to a natural wish to support its unfoldment in others. As with Linda, this may take the form of a natural honoring of the wisdom of others.

It may also take the form of increased sensitivity to school procedures that disrupt the self-connection process. One woman recently told me that since strengthening her connection to her own sense of self, she has become much more aware of situations when disconnection is occurring in a child, and of how often this occurs in school settings. Her reflection reminded me of a particular incident I once witnessed while assisting in a child-care facility. A little girl about six years old was enthusiastically absorbed in an art project of her own design. "I *love* coming here!" she exclaimed to me. When I asked her why, she happily replied, "Because I can *do art* here." Shortly thereafter, the presiding teacher called all the children over for "circle time," insisting that everyone be present. An expression of intense dismay and anguish crossed the little artist's face, and she protested by lingering as long as she could at her project—but in the end she was forced to comply. Though a seemingly small incident, this is an example of profound self-connection disrupted. Because I was familiar with the feeling of deep self-connection she was experiencing, I was able to experience the pain she felt when the connection was abruptly broken.

This incident and others like it have strongly shaped my own thinking and actions with regard to transforming the structure and purposes of education. The example illustrates what can happen when we adults strengthen our connection to our own *querencia* and become more sensitized to disconnection when it occurs in others: we naturally begin to change our own behavior—as well as the system structures—that contribute to disconnection.

Reconnecting—and unfolding the joy

Conrad and Varnum (forthcoming) have documented some of the life changes that have occurred for people who have participated in a workshop designed by Varnum to facilitate connection to their "intuitive knowing." The workshops teach a few simple tools for mastering attention (freeing it from areas where it has gotten stuck or blocked, or from places where it is no longer needed, and redirecting it to where it is desired), thereby enabling participants' attention to go directly to their own joy, life purpose, and destiny.

Evidence from workshop participants demonstrates that (1) the ability to experience profound self-connection can be easily taught and learned, using a few simple tools, in a short period of time; (2) once that connection has been experienced for a sufficient length of time, both internal and external changes can occur with great ease in people's lives; (3) profound self-connection leads to a natural unfoldment of joy, life purpose, and cherished dreams.

My own observations suggest that the more people experience true self-connection, the more they are drawn to use the gifts that grow out of that connection in service to others. It is part of the natural offering of joy that unfolds as people live out their own life purpose. It is then—in blending our own unique talents with service to others—that we experience the "ecstasy and exultation" that Chopra described.

Applying a new model of change

Essentially, I am suggesting that once enough people in schools begin to operate from a new ground of being—the same ground of being we hope to nurture in our school children—real school reform can start to happen. This kind of change can happen in a gentle, transformative way that begins to facilitate wholeness for all involved, a way that shifts the system at a deeper level—at the level of its most basic intention. When we reach a critical mass of adults in schools who are powerfully connected to their own *querencia*, we will begin to see more dramatic shifts in the nature of our schools as well as reductions in our numbers of throw-away children.

The transformational approach I am proposing is premised on principles of change that, although recognized by change theorists and students of transformational studies, are seldom if ever applied in school reform:

1. We are responsible for our own experience and interpretation of reality.
2. External situations are linked to internal conditions, such that anything in our environment that we want to change reflects some energy or tendency that is also present within ourselves (that is, each of us is a hologram of the collective; thus we contain within ourselves all of what appears to be outside us). Therefore, change must begin first with ourselves.
3. Change is not always incremental; it can be large-scale and simultaneous if certain conditions are met.

Central to this approach is an attitude of honoring and respecting all those who are involved in or affected by the change process, especially honoring each person's timing and each person's knowing. Many change efforts engender chaos, confusion, anger, or emotional violence because they seek to impose one person's or one group's will on another. This is contrary to the approach I propose, which views *all of us* as integral parts of one whole. The stance of the change agent in this approach is one of "listening to what is wanting to emerge" and then gently offering it as an option for those who resonate to it (Jaworski, 1996, p. 182).

For individuals, the results of profound self-connection may be dramatic or subtle. Immediate changes may be primarily internal—as in an increased feeling of serenity and composure or a renewed zest for living—or they may be manifested externally. However, over time all internal change eventually results in shifts in the external environment as well. Consequently, if we want to shift the structure and purpose of schools to foster self-connection rather than discourage it, then assisting adults in schools to experience connection *within themselves* offers a powerful potential for school reform.

Achieving the goal

While looking toward fundamental transformation in the long term and on a large scale, it is helpful to also keep the more immediate and local consequences of our work in mind. One of my favorite examples of the effect of the self-connection experience for an individual is the case of a man who participated in one of Varnum's workshops. Throughout the entire four days of the workshop, he said not a word. But as it was ending, he spoke quietly to all the participants: "I haven't said much for these four days. In fact," he added with a chuckle, "I haven't said *anything*. But I want you all to know that I have found my joy" (Varnum, personal communication with the author, July 1997).

When we create schools in such a way that each person in them knows they can go there to find—and live—their joy, then our throw-away children will disappear. They will become, instead, the joyful, productive, engaged, and vital citizenry that all of us, in our hearts, truly desire. Perhaps it is then that as a collective we may begin to experience the joy, rather than the fear, of being our true best self.

References

Callahan, R. *Education and the Cult of Efficiency: A Study of the Social Forces That Have Shaped the Administration of the Public Schools.* Chicago: University of Chicago Press, 1962.

Chopra, D. *The Seven Spiritual Laws of Success: A Practical Guide to the Fulfillment of Your Dreams.* San Rafael, Calif.: Amber-Allen and New World Library, 1993.

Conrad, E. *The Public School Scandal.* New York: John Day, 1951.

Conrad, M., and Varnum, K. *Living the Dream.* Seattle: Pura Vida, forthcoming.

Csikszentmihalyi, M. *Flow: The Psychology of Optimal Experience.* New York: HarperCollins, 1990.

Gatto, J. T. *Dumbing Us Down: The Hidden Curriculum of Compulsory Schooling.* Philadelphia: New Society, 1992.

Jaworski, J. *Synchronicity: The Inner Path of Leadership.* San Francisco: Berrett-Koehler, 1996.

Maslow, A. *The Farther Reaches of Human Nature.* New York: Viking, 1971.

Remen, R. N. *Kitchen Table Wisdom: Stories That Heal.* New York: Riverhead
  Books, 1996.

PAMELA GERLOFF *holds a doctorate in human development from the
Harvard Graduate School of Education. She has taught in schools from
elementary through graduate school levels and is currently an educational
consultant based in Cambridge, Massachusetts.*

Index